The Gift of Allowance

Gary M. Douglas

AC PUBLISHING

The Gift of Allowance
Copyright © 2023 by Gary M. Douglas
ISBN: 978-1-63493-639-2 (paperback)
ISBN: 978-1-63493-640-8 (ebook)

The author and publisher of the book do not make any claim or guarantee for any physical, mental, emotional, spiritual, or financial result. All products, services and information provided by the author are for general education and entertainment purposes only. The information provided herein is in no way a substitute for medical advice. In the event you use any of the information contained in this book for yourself, the author and publisher assume no responsibility for your actions.

Published by Access Consciousness® Publishing
www.acpublishing.com

Contents

Chapter 1:

Allowance

A boy and his aunt are driving down West Main Street in their little town, where the businesses are all lined up on one side and the railroad tracks pass along the other side of the street. East Main Street is the same, and the storefronts face one another over the six sets of rails. As they drive along, the little guy sees the Dairy Bar and says quietly, "I wish I could, but I can't." His head twists around to watch the Dairy Bar go by as his aunt says warmly, "What is it that you wish you could have, but you can't?"

He turns back from the window and says: "A malted milk. A strawberry malted milk."

"You know that you can't have a malted milk, honey. That's way too many calories, and we don't want you to get fat." His aunt drives on, and the boy sits in silence, wishing, just once, that he could have a malted milk.

The following week, the little boy and his aunt are again driving down the street, this time on East Main Street, the other side of the tracks, on their way to the shoe store. Because his feet are so flat, he has to wear what are called "kangaroo shoes," a favorite among police officers, mail carriers, and factory workers who must be on their feet all day. They are high topped shoes, laced to just above the ankle, hardly a fashion statement for a boy, even one with flat feet.

The little boy knows what's coming; he gets new shoes every six months as his feet grow. Because of the special inserts in them, the kangaroo shoes hurt his feet, making him walk on the sides instead of the soles of his feet. He walks, or rather he hobbles, down the hall in school, and the other kids tease him about the way he walks.

As his aunt leads him past the shoe store window, he stops and looks in at a pair of engineer boots. They are the shiny, black boots that all the really cool older boys wear; the tough boys who roll up their shirt sleeves and store a pack of cigarettes in them, and who roll up the cuffs of their tight-fitting Levi's. Just like his big brother. He wants so much to be independent and tough and cool, just like them; just like him.

Nose and hands pressed against the glass, he says to his aunt, "I wish I could, but I can't." To which his aunt replies, "What is it you would like that you can't have?" He explains that he'd like engineer boots, and she says: "You don't want them! The kind of people that wear them aren't like you. They're hoodlums and gangsters! We'll just go and get your shoes. Your special shoes that were made just for you." After she gives him a light tug, he passively follows his aunt into the store. He then climbs into a straight-backed wooden chair, dangling his legs, because they aren't quite long enough to reach the floor, and remains silent as the clerk fits the shoes on his feet.

As the years pass, the little boy stops saying that he wishes he could, but he can't, and it's all forgotten. Now, he simply yearns for things that he wishes he could have or be or do but knows that it's not possible for him.

Without really intending to, the little boy's family indoctrinated him with a number of points of view and judgments about himself and his world. Hoodlums and calories, fat and trouble, judgments based on points of view. And his reaction to these points of view, "I wish I could, but I can't," became a fixed point of view for him, one he'd use instead of asking directly for something. As a result of all of this, he stopped wishing and he stopped asking, all of which made him burn inside. The points of view became part of his personality and played a significant role in the way he lived his life. Of course, others contributed to the formation of these

7

and other points of view, such as the kids ridiculing him, making sure that he knew he was different, hence unacceptable, or the junior high school girls who didn't respond well to his asking: "I don't suppose you'd want to go to the movies with me."

"I wish; I can't" became the foundation for most of what happened to this boy later in life. Sometimes he'd rage in despair, because he never seemed to have the things he wanted and was tired of settling for what others permitted him to have.

How many times have you experienced "I wish I could, but I know I can't" in your life? Have you tried to make things different or better a hundred different ways, but nothing seemed to work, or if it did work, it was never what you thought it would be?

While you tried to write it off as the unfairness of the world, the problem always seemed to be that there was something "wrong" with you deep down inside and, no matter how hard you tried, you couldn't make it right. "Rightness" became the strawberry malt and the engineer boots that were right there in front of you, but always out of reach. In the tale of the little boy, when he wanted something for himself, he was presented with a point of view and a judgment. You can't have a strawberry malted milk; it will make you fat, and fat is bad. Nice boys don't get fat. Engineer boots are only for bad people; nice people don't wear them. A point of view is given and followed with a judgment.

A judgment can be defined as any point of view that a person agrees or aligns with or resists or reacts to. Whose points of view, with the attached judgments, have you been using to create your life? What must you do, or must you never do? Do you know? The little boy had no idea that he was being infused with the points of view of those around him. He just knew that he couldn't have engineer boots and that those boots would become central to his points of view about a group of people he considered to be hoodlums.

It isn't necessary to live one's life like a ping-pong ball, ever at the mercy of other people's points of view and judgments. The problem isn't that other people's judgments or points of view are stronger or "righter" than yours; it is that you are unaware of what is really happening. The little boy was unaware that he had aligned with the "engineer boots are for hoodlums" point of view. He just knew that he couldn't have boots or, seemingly, anything else he wanted in life. To live differently takes both awareness and the willingness to allow yourself to *be*. To BE! To exist as YOU, not as a mixture of other people's thoughts on who and what you must be.

Under the assumption that it is a person's *wrongness* that is the root of their unhappiness, the majority of people are more interested in being right than in being themselves and being free to choose the life that actually works for them. Instead of going out to buy his boots, as an adult, the little boy judges those who wear them as bad or wrong. The point of view that he learned as a child took root and he made it a part of himself.

Rather than enjoying the possibilities life has to offer, people seek to be perfect, which is to say, always right. They spend great energy and enormous time on being perfect, bending their world to fit the "right way." Since everyone seems to have their own point of view about right and wrong, it becomes an exercise in futility. Does this create a life that inspires people, or makes them happy?

What if people could stop trying to be perfect, or allowed themselves to be wrong in light of their fixed points of view? The willingness to be wrong and make mistakes, or to break from established points of view, allows you to be aware of choices that other people might not even consider. Post-it® Notes came about after a chemist mistakenly made a glue that didn't stick right. How would you post your "Out to Lunch" notices without the little yellow sticky note, created by mistake? There are a lot more possibilities to be found in the scrap pile of attempts than on the shelf of successes. But you can only get to them if you are able to allow yourself to make a mistake. From there you can choose what action you would like to take next based on the awareness of your actions.

It is awareness, not judgment of right and wrong, that is essential for the creation of a thriving, successful life and world. With total awareness, you have the freedom to choose and create beyond the limitations everybody else thinks are real and true. Without total awareness, you can't have total creation of the life you desire.

To have awareness of what each action creates, you must be willing to move beyond the definitions of everything you have judged to be right and wrong. For example, you might have to give up a lifelong attachment to the awfulness of the world in order to live from a place of joy. Surprisingly, many people are much more attracted to, or perhaps addicted to, the woes of the world than they are to the prospect of living joyously.

With your judgments, you cut off your awareness; you don't see that which does not fit your judgment. We are told to think outside the box. The irony here is that we create the boxes we're trying to think outside of! They're called judgments. If you drive a white car, it seems that parking lots are absolutely full of white cars. You don't even really see the red or blue ones, because you've quietly aimed your attention at white. In other words, when you judge something as right or wrong, you are putting on blinders that block out everything that does not match your point of view. However, when you function without judgment, the blinders come off, and, out of the blue, doors begin to open up around you that create possibilities you may never have considered.

Most of us have been trained from the time we were little to come to judgments and conclusions about everything. This is all part of the addiction to rightness and wrongness that we've been using to limit the choices available to us. The key to moving beyond all of this is *allowance*.

Allowance is about what you're willing to receive. It includes everything and judges nothing. When you are "in allowance," you never have to have a point of view about whether something is right or wrong, good or bad. Every point of view that you are aware of is just an *"interesting point of view."* It is awareness that turns a point of view from a judgment to simply a passing opinion that won't stick to you. If you are not in allowance, you cannot receive all that you are aware of because you can only judge what you must reject and what you will align with. This means you will push whatever does not match your judgments and conclusions out of your reality. Everything that you desire to receive must pass through your personal censors before you can receive it. Allowance removes this board of stern-faced, black-robed, sour judges, and allows you to receive everything.

When you are in total allowance you can receive everything—the good, the bad, and the ugly. Because you do not have to have a point of view or judgment about what you are aware of, every single, solitary particle of information becomes available to you. When you can be aware of anything, you can change anything. When you can change anything, you can have total success with all that you create.

For example, some people have been taught that violence is wrong and should be avoided at all costs. It is interesting to note that when people describe others who are violent, they usually do so from a place of anger, and start imagining the kinds of brutal punishment the violent person should receive. If confronted with their reaction as an expression of violence, the person will deny it, because they can't see it. The judgments people carry about violence can blind them to their own violence.

Defining violence as right or wrong is, simply, a judgment. Violence, no matter what point of view you may take about it, is a part of the world. If you have decided that violence is wrong, you may choose not to see all the forms it takes or push what you have defined as violent out of your world. If you have the point of view that violence is wrong, how likely are you to acknowledge where you or a loved one may be violent? Defining violence as right creates a similar set of blinders. If a person is conditioned to deal with problems through violence, nonviolent solutions will disappear into the night, leading the person to meet challenges regarding their "authority or power" forcefully; violently.

There are situations in which choosing something that one person may consider to be violent could create greater possibilities. A woman has finally tired of being treated unfairly in her job and, one day, she stands up and screams, "That's it! I've had all I'm going to take!" She pushes the contents of her desk onto the floor and marches out of the office. Her shocked coworkers could say that this was an unnecessarily violent scene. She, on the other hand, might see it as having been freed to look at the possibilities of a larger world. Nice girls don't make violent scenes. So, in order to be nice, she stagnates in a swamp she hates. Whether she was right or wrong to do what she did all depends on whose point of view, whose judgment you're listening to.

What would your life be like if you chose to be aware of anything and everything without having to judge the rightness or wrongness of your awareness? Would you make different choices? What would be possible for you to create that you have not yet chosen?

CHAPTER 2:

It All Starts With an Interesting Point of View

G oing back to the little boy's aunt telling him that engineer boots are for hoodlums and gangsters, the point of view that he developed about the boots became truth for him. He would fight a bear to defend his acquired point of view that only hoodlums wore engineer boots. What would have happened if he recognized that what his aunt told him was simply her *interesting point of view*? In order to become totally aware, it is necessary to recognize that every point of view, yours or others', is just an interesting point of view. It is neither right nor wrong, good nor bad.

If you really want to get free to create a greater life and world, allow yourself to acknowledge all of the *interesting points of view* you are aware of. Each time you notice a point of view, simply repeat the phrase, "Interesting point of view that this person has this point of view," or "interesting point of view that I have this point of view," until the energy of the point of view shifts. It's a bit like thinking that your car's engine is completely shot and then finding that the error was in the computer the mechanic was using, and there's really nothing wrong with your engine. Compare the amount of energy you experienced as tension during that dead engine part of the conversation and the release of that energy as tension when you found out your car was okay. Allowance changes the energy we experience. We all experience energy, often without thought or recognition except when there is a discernable change in it. Interesting point of view allows for changes in energy.

While people who begin living from an "interesting point of view" often experience some change right away, people who have practiced this for 6 months until it became a habit, experienced huge changes. If you commit to this practice, you will likely discover how many fixed points of view you have used to create your life as it is now. This is not to imply that your life right now is somehow wrong or bad. You might be happy and content.

However, even if you are satisfied with your life, it might be interesting to see how it could be expanded simply by getting rid of the judgments you do carry. Ask yourself, "What judgments and fixed points of view do I have that limit the amount of joy I could be experiencing?" How do you change your life? Just realize that it's based on "simply an interesting point of view that I have this point of view."

"I can't get out of debt!" is an interesting point of view that allows you to bring into your life those things that will enable you to be in debt. "I just can't get into a relationship!" Really? Interesting point of view that you have that point of view! How many possible relationships have you blinded yourself to, living from a fixed point of view that you can't have one? Or how many really wonderful relationships were sabotaged because they were too good to be true! Our fixed points of view and judgments are the truths of our limited existence, but not necessarily the truth.

When you are functioning from a place of everything simply being an interesting point of view, you have no *fixed* points of view. Everything is just a point of view you have taken for the moment; it doesn't hold any meaning, and you can change it. And when you can change in any direction in a heartbeat, with no point of view, the possibilities available for you to choose show up. Until you relax your stranglehold on your points of view, your only choice in life is either to align and agree or resist and react to the world around you.

Whenever we align and agree with a point of view, we make it correct and buy it as a point of view to function from. The opposite is also true. Whenever we resist or react, we have to first give credence to the point of view before we can set ourselves up to reject it. Consider how much energy you have spent agreeing with or fighting against everyone else's points of view. What might be possible for you if you were to recognize that every single point of view is an invention and not an eternal truth? What would your life be like if you chose to simply be in allowance of all points of view? If you have no point of view, you can have *all* points of view. If you have all points of view, then you have infinite possibilities. You can be, do, have, create, and generate anything.

What does it mean to have all points of view? Think about how, the moment you take a point of view, you begin to set your world up around that point of view. For example, if you have decided that being "nice" is an important way to be, you have to judge the relative niceness of any possible action before you can choose. You make yourself the "nice" character in the story of your life. If, however, you are willing to have all points of view, you become the author of your story rather than one particular character in the story. As the author, you can be aware of all the characters and the many ways in which each character functions. From that space of awareness of the many points of view of each and every character around you, you can begin to choose whatever action will create greater possibilities. You will no longer be limited to the points of view of one particular character. This space of awareness is what opens up the freedom to truly create whatever you desire.

If you engage in alignment and agreement, or resistance and reaction, you get caught up in the stream of life and get washed away. If you are in allowance, however, you do not have to take any particular point of view. You can be the rock in the stream of life that all energies flow around. You can be aware of all the points of view without having to be pushed or pulled by them. You want to be that which allows everything to just go around you. It's all just an interesting point of view.

When you function from interesting point of view, there is a different possibility available in all things. This requires awareness. It is important to realize those times when you are doing allowance and the times when you are doing alignment and agreement or resistance and reaction. Once you become aware of the difference, you may be surprised at the ways in which you have chosen to interact with other people's points of view.

Alignment and agreement is happening when you walk up to somebody who has been yelled at and put your arm around them to give them comfort. That is alignment and agreement with their point of view, not allowance for them to change. In so doing, you solidify the rightness of their point of view—which is why they chose to do whatever they did in the first place. Your choice to agree with them can actually stick them with holding onto the point of view they chose. There are other options. For example, from an interesting point of view, a person might just listen and reflect, allowing the upset person to talk and reason out his own choices and their effects.

A little girl came running into the kitchen, crying. She clung to her mother and sobbed: "Suzie was mean to me! She hit me and it hurt!" The mother is confronted with the little girl's point of view that she had been victimized by the girl next door. If she buys into that point of view, along with it come the judgments that her daughter is helpless and unable to resolve differences with her playmate, that mother must fix this situation so that her daughter won't feel bad, that the girl next door is bad, and more. However, when being interesting point of view, an infinite number of other paths open up, because she doesn't need to choose the "sheltering my daughter!" path. In this case, the mother chose to be interesting point of view and replied: "Yes, but you're bigger than she is…" The girl responded, "That's right! I am!", turned around and ran from the house. It's interesting to note that the two girls were playing amicably within about five minutes. Of course, there are an infinite number of possible outcomes here, but there would have been far fewer had the mother created, "Bad Suzie, poor little daughter" by buying into the *helpless little girl* point of view.

Allowance requires you to question everything. When faced with the above scenario, rather than running to comfort the person who has been yelled at or turning the friend of the little girl into "Bad Suzie," try using interesting point of view: "Interesting point of view they have this point of view." "Interesting point of view I have this point of view."

Why does somebody have this point of view? And why do they think they're right? Again, most people want to be right and don't care what it takes to get the rightness of their point of view.

Two friends, with decidedly different world views, are driving down a country road when one says:

"Look, there is a black cow!"

The other replies: "I don't see a black cow."

"It's right there, in the pasture, plain as can be. A black cow!"

"I think you're wrong. There isn't a black cow in the pasture. I do see a cow that is black on this side; I don't know what color it is on the other side, so I wouldn't necessarily call it a black cow."

Who's right? It all depends on the point of view.

Where is the rightness in *any* point of view? An individual's point of view derives rightness by way of his or her judgment; they have judged it to be so, and so it is! Rightness is simply a judgment. More often than not, people use the rightness of their point of view to confirm the wrongness of others, or even of themselves. For example, listen in as two people discuss different religions. Those discussions can get pretty intense, because both participants will claim that their rightness is derived from The Creator. They both try to change the thinking of the other person in order to put them on the "path of truth and light." How can that be if they are both quoting the same source? Many religions are about right and wrong, with their doctrines mandating "right" answers and disavowing "wrong" answers for its followers. Does any of it have to do with what's just or what's true? If it does, from whose point of view is that determined?

Total allowance is realizing that your point of view is just your point of view. It doesn't make you right, and it doesn't make you wrong. Ask yourself, "How are my points of view limiting me? How are my points of view creating what I am not happy with?" A mathematician once gave a lecture to a large group of people. During the course of his talk, he asked how many of the participants were "dumb in math." He was stunned when all but a few people raised their hands. That is just not statistically possible. Most of the people raising their hands had judged themselves or were judged to be "dumb in math" and as a result, they made choices in their lives based on their math judgment that would prove to themselves and the world that they are dumb in math. Instead of being an astronaut, as they dreamed of when they were children, they had to settle for something else because they knew, in their heart of hearts, that they didn't have what it takes. They were dumb in math.

What if they asked themselves, "Am I so dumb in math?" "How do I know?" "That's an interesting point of view, and it's an interesting point of view that I have that point of view." And that's all it takes. Points of view create what you are not happy with. They are simultaneously the reason, justification, and source for your unhappiness.

When you choose to make a point of view valuable, you set the stage to judge anything—and most frequently yourself—as right or wrong based on that point of view. What if there was no right and no wrong? What if everything was just an interesting point of view? You can either be in allowance or sit in judgment. Please know that you always have a choice.

CHAPTER 3:

Are Judgments Real?

William Shakespeare, in his comedy *As You Like It*, writes:

All the world's a stage,
And all the men and women merely players;
They have their exits and their entrances,
And one man in his time plays many parts…

The title of this play, its opening lines, and the fact that it is a play, all seem to fit into the subject of choice. *As You Like It* suggests that you get to choose whatever life you'd like to live: good, bad, right or wrong. Shakespeare wrote a little of each, from comedies to tragedies. He supposes that the world, or perhaps this reality, is a stage upon which people can play the parts they have chosen for themselves and switch parts as they wish.

Even if we're not aware of them, we make choices all the time. We read this magazine instead of that one in the dentist's office. An article we read starts us thinking of what we can be and what we can't be, based on the existing judgments of ourselves. I could do that! I could never do that!

What led us to that chair? To that dentist? We choose all of the points of view about ourselves and about our world, even though we seldom acknowledge the choices. Collectively, these points of view define our realities. When we choose our points of view and slip them on like shoes, we create the "players" we become. The points of view we choose, our own or others', will be based on a judgment. Think about it. "You've got to work hard to get ahead. If you don't, you'll never get any place," and that becomes your point of view about working. Once that's in place, you will choose the things that support the point of view about working hard. "He drinks a bit and kicks his dog, but he's a hard worker!" Hard work becomes the measure of the person. It's okay if he's a jerk or if he's a mean-spirited rat. If he works hard, he's got some redeeming social value. What if life didn't take hard work in order to be wonderful?

If those choices define our realities, who's doing the choosing? Is there a "you" that is offstage, unaffected by the points of view the character represents? Indeed there is, although the "players" are unaware of that person and will resist the awareness of that being, in an attempt to continue living in their self-made realities. Should a person in this position start becoming aware, awakening from the point of view trance, the restraints start to drop away. How do we rid ourselves of the roles we play and simply become ourselves free of judgment? By awareness of ourselves and the world. The more you use the tool "interesting point of view" the more your awareness expands, enabling you to more clearly perceive the subtle energies that shape each moment, which in turn can help you recognize where you are prioritizing points of view and judgments over awareness.

Judgments solidify energy, stop possibilities and shape people's realities. When "in judgment," instead of creating the things we desire, we create blocks that prevent us from receiving them. There is a paradox here in that it doesn't matter whether the judgment is about good and right, or bad and wrong. Either way, the effect is the same: solidified energy and limited possibilities. Consider for a moment where you have had a judgment thrown at you, such as, "You just can't do anything right!"

An inexperienced server in a restaurant spills soup on a customer. Embarrassed, the server grabs a towel and apologizes over and over to the customer, who doesn't say anything out loud, but glowers. Later, the server loses an order slip, and a different customer waits for an order that wasn't placed. The cook wails, "Can't you do anything right? What's wrong with you? Are you stupid or what?" Shamed and embarrassed again, the server shrinks inside and tries to get things right, only to make more mistakes. And so it goes for the rest of the shift.

If you were the server, would you buy the judgment as real and true? Was it believable to you that you are unable to do anything right and there's something wrong with you, or you're stupid? If so, did you agree that you are somehow "damaged goods," or disagree with the judgment? If you agreed with it, the next time you look for a job, this judgment will likely run in your mind the times that you made a mess of things, remembering them with great clarity and even feeling the residual shame and self-recrimination. How many jobs that would be a good fit for you would you avoid because of this judgment?

If you disagreed, you might find yourself being defensive and angry that anyone could think that of you. You would perhaps think of all the times you did great things that disprove the judgment as you project defiance at the person who interviews you. How many lies do you tell yourself about all the incompetent people out there who can't see your greatness?

The point here is that, whether you agreed or disagreed, the energetic outcome will be the same—the energy that shows up as you are accusing yourself or defending yourself "solidifies," creating a situation where judgment is always in front of you, preventing you from creating other things in your life. You either look for or take a job that might be perfect for you, only to have the weight of this judgment burden you, causing you to fall into old "can't do anything right" patterns.

If you simply ask a question whenever a judgment is directed at you rather than instantly buying it and supporting it, the judgment doesn't take root. Is this true about me? Am I truly incapable?

What if you could be in allowance of yourself and look at the energy of the moment? Instead of shaming yourself, which feels dark and heavy and awful, you could look from a place of simply seeing what is going on as an interesting point of view. You probably could clean up the soup, mollify the customer and go on with your life, not dragging the incident behind you like a can tied to a dog's tail.

This is what it is like to lose your ability to choose your reality to a fixed point of view based on a judgment. By aligning yourself with the judgment that you must never make a mistake, such as losing a customer order, you lose the very things that you wanted to be or have.

Let's change the picture a little. Instead of aligning and agreeing with the judgment about stupidity and clumsiness, making them real and true, let's respond differently. At the moment that the judgment about stupidity and "can't do anything right" shows up, let's recognize it as simply someone's point of view. It would pass around you or through you, but it would not stick. There would be no solidification of the energy of the judgment because you saw it for what it was: simply an interesting point of view.

Finding the way out of being a target for judgments could be as simple as asking a question whenever a judgment is directed at you. Is this real? Is this based on truth or something else? When you are in allowance, you buy no judgments, and you are able to truly see yourself and your world clearly. When you are in allowance, willing to *be where and what you are at the moment* with no point of view, you can choose anything. You will not be limited to the judgments and points of view you are presented with, and you can then start asking, what do I really want to choose? Do I want to dedicate my life to expressing a judgment, mine or someone else's, or would I rather learn how to live my life joyously and with ease and maybe enjoying the work that I do without the heaviness of compulsion obstructing me? What's really going to make a difference?

To get out of the grasp of judgment, it is necessary to realize that the moment you buy a judgment as something real, you have to cut off your awareness in order to keep the judgment as a reality. You have to willingly choose stupidity, which according to the dictionary, can be defined as "the suspension of intelligence, understanding, reason, or wit," in order to believe that a judgment is real. We have to dismiss everything we know to be true and dismiss everything that is possible for us in order to have that belief. Any time you choose to believe a judgment, stop and ask yourself, "How stupid can I be here?" "How much intelligence, understanding, reason, or wit, can I suspend?" For that is really what we are doing; we are creating ourselves as stupid enough to believe that judgment is real.

We use judgments as a means to avoid having our own awareness. Like the petunia in the onion patch, we are alone and stick out when set among people who are in judgment, a frightening experience for some because we can't turn to anyone but ourselves for verification.

Our choices look different if they are totally *ours*. If we simply choose rather than gathering a consensus of other people's judgments, we find ourselves surrounded by possibilities.

When living from allowance rather than judgment, you begin to feel a deep serenity or ease with yourself that significantly alters the way you appear to people. You no longer react to judgments or fixed points of view but maintain within yourself the calmness from knowing that it's all an interesting point of view. A fantasy used to control you. From the other side of this interaction, where a person controls through judgments and fixed points of view, there is the expectation of a reaction. If you don't react to judgment, why judge you? In the end you get written off as a lost cause, that is, unable to be manipulated and controlled, and the last-ditch judgments are cast at you. The person judging accuses you overtly or covertly with the point of view that you have changed because you are frightened, or aloof, or somehow deficient. That person defines you as too small and insignificant to succeed without their input.

What is the allure of judgment? People judge one another in a game of "I'm taller and more powerful than you," or "you can't hurt me," or some other existential competition designed to create a sense of power in the one judging. You might notice that you feel more powerful when you judge someone. If you judge them as good or right, you are superior and look down on them to praise. If you judge them as bad or wrong, you are the Master who can dole out punishment. Because they can rely on a judgment, they don't have to choose whether something is right or good or bad or wrong for themselves—it's already written in the judgments by which they live. Is a person more powerful because he's decided that the person next to him or her is lacking? Is that power the most important thing in life? It seems so when people judge. People who judge are able to exclude anybody they want to, often to their loss. There is a price for judgment.

If you never had to believe any judgment, would you be willing to let go of all of the places that you've decided, determined, judged, and concluded that you must believe in judgment? If you gave up all the judgments you've used to create your world, only you would remain, only *you*, free to be aware and to choose and create the life you desire.

It is true that judgement is all around us, but just because so many are choosing it does not mean that it is the only choice available. That so many choose to act as though judgment is real does not mean that you have to; nor do you have to believe that it *is* real. Because someone has posted online that women who are taller than 5'6" are likely to be more successful, are they? If you are shorter than that, are you inferior? Must you apologize for being what you are? Or are you buying into a bunch of nonsense? It would be great to have an expert guide to help you along with sorting this out. The good news is that you have one already! It's you! And if you ask yourself a question such as "is this true?", your body and mind will answer. If it's heavy, it's a lie, and light is truth. Take something that has stuck you and made you feel bad, that is a lie, when you look at the energy of lies, they are stagnant. A lighter feeling is what is true for you, something that makes you happy, brings you joy, this is the energy of truth.

Unfortunately, it seems that the most important thing for many people is to never have too much awareness. You might have noticed that people often carry a mixed desire to be both exceptional and inobtrusive. If they become aware, they may no longer be able to carry their point of view that they are unique. Or they may fear that, if they stand out, someone will actually see them, which can be interpreted as judging them. In this dilemma lies the fear of being aware. It seems safer to hide behind the curtain of unawareness, even though there is a price to pay for it. That is the primary reason so many people choose judgments. With judgment, you don't have to be aware; and as long as you are unaware, you can have a difficult life full of trauma and drama, just like everyone else. If you are aware, you just might find that you are unique.

I have not yet found anyone who could give an answer to the question of what makes judgment real. I have been given reasons and justifications for judgments. I have been told why they should exist, and what people expect to get out of them, or what judgments will protect people from, but that's not what makes judgment real. All of those reasons and justifications for the judgment are the lies people use to distort their universe, so that they can be unaware enough to become a victim of it. Where are you choosing unawareness and victimhood over the allowance and awareness that would make all of your life more expansive, more successful, and more joyful?

Do you have any idea what an expansive, successful, joyful life would be?

Here is where you get to practice honing your energetic awareness to explore what is true for you—not what is right or wrong, but what creates a sense of ease and joy.

The life and world that works for you is one that lights you up and brings a smile to your face. It is light and creative, rather than heavy, and ponderous. In general, however, people are taught to give value to that which is heavy, intense and significant rather than that which has a sense of space and possibilities to it. If you look for it, you'll see that we surround ourselves with that value: we read heavy books, attend heavy movies, we have deep and heavy conversations. We value intensity and heaviness, describing it as significant, thinking that these increase our stature, and that lightness and joy are frippery. "Can't you ever be serious?", said with a frown. "Can't you ever be joyous?", the smiling response.

Please note that not every judgment is "negative." And not every awareness is "positive." In fact, the same words can be used to judge someone *or* to acknowledge an awareness. For example, you could say that someone is "messy." If you say this with a point of view about the messiness, therein lies the judgment. You could, however, point out that a person has a messy home or a messy appearance without having any charge or point of view attached. Some people are simply messier than others. That is not a problem. Nor is it a rightness. It is simply an awareness. To some, this awareness may appear to be negative. Yet it is simply an acknowledgment of what is.

Take a look at your life. Have you ever avoided being aware of anything that seemed "negative"? For example, have you avoided being aware that someone you know is a liar or a cheat? Though these words may appear to be a negative judgment, they may also accurately describe the energy from which someone is functioning.

There might be an intensity bordering on aggressiveness that makes you want to buy into a story. This is the "selling the sale" part of making a judgment "purchase"—never mind the man behind the curtain! We can blind ourselves to all kinds of craziness if we ignore our awareness.

At the other end of the spectrum are the positive judgments. Surprisingly, these can be even stickier than the negative judgments, as people are often less willing to let go of the "positive" than they are the "negative." For example, let's say that you have decided someone you know is a good person. What points of view are you using to eliminate any contradictions to this? Are you willing to look at the persons "negative" qualities, or do you justify them, conveniently making them not exist? What if you didn't have to have any points of view about liars, cheats, messy people, good people, or anyone else? What if you could drop the lens of judgment through which you've been observing the world and see everything for what it is, in each moment, regardless of anyone's points of view?

In general, a judgment has an intensity to it. Whereas an awareness makes you feel lighter, even if it's negative. You've got to be willing to see the judgment and see the awareness. But as long as you're willing to believe that a judgment is real, you must turn your back on your awareness. If you choose to believe that the invented reality of a judgment is real, you will not allow yourself to know the difference between a judgment and an awareness.

Nothing that anyone judges is real or true. It's just an opinion and has no value to you. You have to be in allowance of yourself and your awareness, no matter what judgments come your way. Judgments are simply not true. They are merely points of view with a charge to them. Let's say somebody says to you, "You're really screwed up!" Rather than wondering if you *are* screwed up or how you are screwed up, simply ask, "Is that true?" Notice the energy. Use the tool "interesting point of view." And see what you discover. You do not have to make any judgment a reality.

Yet judgment as a reality is a creation that most people have chosen in order to prove that we have a reality. We'd rather have a reality than an awareness. We'd rather buy someone else's point of view than have our own awareness, because that way we can fit in, even though we don't fit in. It's crazy! And it is what the majority of people are choosing.

If you would actually like to create greater possibilities, you've got to look at these things. You've got to be willing to be present, and you've got to be willing to choose. Judgment/reality might be compared to riding a bus through a beautiful forest with a guide telling you what you are seeing and when to say, "Ooh! Aaah!" Awareness is being allowed to walk through the forest with the freedom to walk where you'd like. Sometimes you walk through a patch of beautiful, fragrant flowers and sometimes through a smelly bog, teeming with life. You get to choose where you'd like to go and what you'd like to experience.

Recognize whose points of view you have been following and whose you have not. Why do you reject some judgments and swallow others? What if it were all just an interesting point of view, even the judgments *you* have had?

Remember that judgment is just judgment. It's not true. Judgments don't change anything. And they don't make anything better. Recognize where you are trying to create your reality based on the judgments other people are using to create theirs. Be kind to you! Be kind to the world! Challenge yourself to be a source of different possibilities in the world. If you didn't have judgment from which to create your world and reality, what would you choose?

CHAPTER 4:

What Do You Truly Desire to Create?

A woman left her career when her child was born. Her husband had a good job, and they were financially secure. After she left the company, she threw her energy into being a stay-at-home mom, active in all of the usual parent activities at home and in school and at play. She didn't forget herself; she actively kept her mind sharp at book club and cultural events. Once her child entered high school, she found that there were fewer demands on her time, and she recognized a desire to expand into the greater world in a meaningful way. She decided to go back to work.

Dusting off forgotten skills, she created a resume and put together her work history to present for prospective employers. Her work history was something about which she could be proud. It was actually a bit of a shock for her to see what her accomplishments had been.

When she completed her resume, she began looking for places to send it. She checked out all of the companies she could think of that might be similar to the one she left, which was no longer in business. She looked at former competitors and other companies whose names she looked up on the Internet. Those she knew about were no longer in business, had moved to another state or another country, or had been bought out by a larger company and "swallowed up." Starting to get a bit concerned, she turned to her friend, a savvy businesswoman, for a bit of advice and encouragement.

After reading the woman's resume, her friend had some comments. She pointed out how strong the woman's past history was and marveled at the things she had accomplished and what her skill set was. Toward the end of that discussion, the friend pointed out to her what she felt was a glaring omission. She noticed that the woman had failed to include her strengths and assets – almost as though she was afraid that people would think that she was bragging.

When they talked about it, the woman was almost apologetic about the things she did well, brushing them aside and diminishing them during the conversation. The friend, bewildered, asked her if she would take ownership of all the marvelous things she is and does, but nothing was really resolved.

The conversation ended in a discussion about the question: "Is this the job you want?" The more they talked about that, the more it became apparent that the woman had a very narrow view of the job she was trying to find. Rather than looking for the job where she could create and express herself and grow, she just wanted a job that matched her picture of her past job. And, because she was unwilling to recognize her amazing abilities and what she could do with them, she truly didn't know what she desired in her work or in her life.

Instead of exploring the life that she'd really like, she found herself picking through the possibilities that others had demonstrated or suggested, whether they brought joy or not. She was not aware that she had given away the life she wanted for what she judged to be a life acceptable to others. Her life was being run by the points of view and judgments of others, rather than by her own desires. These friends were giving her judgments with the best of intentions but, they were judgments, nonetheless. She started to become aware of her situation by having some talks with herself about the influences that affected her view of what she could do or be. It was incredibly revealing!

Take a moment to get present with the points of view you are using to create the life you are presently living. You might notice that many of those points of view didn't originate with you, like trying to do what everybody else is doing, or what your parents, teachers, spouse, or peers told you to do. Are there any points of view that you have been functioning from that simply are not working for you? Trying to live from the idea that if you could just do the "right" thing, you would finally have the "right" kind of life. Where did *that* point of view come from? Trying to do what is right is a bit nebulous—everybody's got a different definition of right which seems to be pretty fuzzy as a guide to living. Right is also a judgment as is its opposite, wrong. So, what choices are you making based on that point of view?

It is the choices you are making in every moment that create the direction your life is heading. Ultimately, you've got to be aware of when you're choosing and what your choices actually are. However, there is a difference between being aware of choices and judging them. Being aware simply means that you know they are there. It's like opening the curtains and seeing everything that's outside your window. When you judge your choices, you limit your awareness of those choices.

If you are unwilling to be aware of the choices you are making, you set yourself up to be a victim of the life you are creating. What would be possible if you acknowledged your choices, good or bad, or right or wrong, with the awareness that they were simply choices. The marvelous thing about choices is that if it turns out that you don't like your choice, you can make another one.

Where choices become difficult is when the weight of judgment is introduced to them. What if it's the wrong choice? What if I fail? Doubt creeps into the choice, eating away at your joy and enthusiasm, until the choice is dark and heavy. What if you chose to be in allowance of your choices instead of coming to conclusion about whether they are right or wrong or good or bad? Your choices could be "simply an interesting point of view" and instead of judging them, you could be present with the choices you are making, and you would not see them perverted by a point of view.

What if you allowed yourself to be vulnerable about your choices? It sounds kind of odd, and most people react negatively to the idea that they might benefit from being vulnerable. In this case, vulnerability does not mean being a target for someone or something trying to do you harm; vulnerability is that space of having no barrier to anything. When you have no barrier to anything, you can receive everything. Through vulnerability, you can allow yourself to be aware of all energies. How can you see your choice come into being if you surround yourself with a heavy suit of armor? Are there any energies that you have been avoiding or reacting to, or are there energies that you have been allowing to dominate your choices? If you use "interesting point of view" around your choices, you allow all the energy, all the possibilities, to come to your awareness because there is no wall of judgment impeding them.

You might think of it this way. If each energy were a color, what color palettes have you been using to create the work of art that is your life? Have you used judgments to limit the colors of energy you can create with? When you choose to be in allowance, you open your perception to the limitless colors of every energy that is available for you to choose. And when you no longer force yourself to limit the colors you choose, your creations can take on a vibrancy and resonance that reflects the masterful creator you truly *can* be...not the paint-by-numbers follower you've been pretending to be.

"That person really thinks outside the box!" The box in question is made of judgments and fixed points of view. From inside the box, it is unlikely you will be creative, because when you reach out with your energy for awareness, it is repelled by a wall of judgment. If you cannot be aware of everything that's going on, you cannot truly create.

Suppose you would like to choose a new situation in your life. A skill, or a job, or healing, just a choice. If you would like to have something specific in your life, or in the world, start by asking, "How can I be in allowance with this?" You must first have allowance that this is what you would like to create. Not that it's right or wrong. Not that it's good or bad. Not that this is what you have to do. But simply that this is what you would like to create.

Does the possibility of being the masterful creator of your life appeal to you? If so, you can begin by being honest with yourself as you uncover the points of view you have been using to create your world. Think of the judgments that you have turned into virtues and rightness so others will think you are a good – right – person, the judgments that you use to keep yourself on the straight and narrow! If you don't do that you surely won't succeed. There might be a very large number of such points of view operating in your life, keeping you from living a life of choice. Look each in the face and simply be aware that they are there. Be in allowance of them. A reminder about the definition of allowance here: be willing to experience everything and judge nothing.

What would it be like if, instead of living as the effect of anything outside of you, you knew you could get anywhere you wanted to get, you could create whatever you wanted to create whenever you wanted to create it, and you could have whatever you wanted to have? Would you be willing to be that successful?

CHAPTER 5:

What Are You Willing to Do or Be?

M ost people's lives are directed by a "rule book" filled with judgments. The judgments are broad in scope, from those that define you to those that define your whole world. People talk to themselves more often than they talk to others. It would be an interesting exercise to pay attention to what's being said in your head. "That's too hard." "I'm afraid of…" "Remember the time you offended your boss? That was awful!" The point here is not that you'd think such things; the point is that you react to them, judge them, and use them to create your life. You don't pick things that you have decided are too hard to do based on your judgments, even if you've never tried them. You react to the fears in your mind by avoiding the causes of them.

You always watch your speech, to make sure that you never offend anyone. It seems as though there are an infinite number of rules for you to obey just getting from one day to the next.

Your life can be greater by far, simply by letting go of this circle of rules or judgments. The question is, how much judgment can you go beyond to create a reality that actually works for you? It is important to acknowledge again and again that the world so many of us have grown up in is based on judgments and fixed points of view, rather than on awareness. If those self-limiting thoughts are disposed of, what is left? Possibilities.

The unwillingness to look at different possibilities limits what you can create. If you have determined that you have a morbid fear of speaking in public, you limit the number of possibilities that might involve speaking to a group or an auditorium or a national audience. You are left with the small world of your fears, which is to say, points of view or judgments, with the same old trauma and drama that everyone else is choosing. The possibilities leave this world because your "judgment rules" won't allow you to choose them.

The change needed to live a fuller life can begin immediately. Choosing to step out of judgment and into allowance can start with simply allowing for judgment itself. What if you could be in allowance of your judgments, looking at each as simply an interesting point of view? "It is an interesting point of view that I am afraid of speaking to people." As soon as you recognize that fear for what it is, the energy of the fear moves away from you and what is left is you—without fear. Pay attention to all of the judgments you have been functioning from. Taking each judgment or fixed point of view individually, without judging yourself about having them, and seeing them as interesting points of view, can free you from them instead of using them to define yourself and your world. Instead of using these judgments to stifle your creations, this will allow you to acknowledge what is required to create whatever you desire.

Suppose that you are building a house. The first thing you'll do is dig a hole for the foundation of the house. Once the hole is dug you have…a hole. That's great, however, some other things need to take place before you have a house. It's time to start building. Unloading a big mound of judgments is the equivalent of digging the hole for the foundation. You don't stop there, unless you wish to live in a hole.

Having rid yourself of judgments, it's time to make some choices. Thinking about the job or the relationships or the money or the health you'd like to have, you ask questions such as "What would it take for me to have that job?" "To be in total health?" "To have more money than I can spend?"

The energy seems right for this or that, so you have found what you'd really like, based on YOU. The next step, then, is to create that life.

In order to create the life you desire, you've got to be willing to be whatever it takes to become everything you wish to become, with no point of view. It doesn't require a point of view; it just requires a choice. Let's say you made a choice to be happy. The world is filled with people who are frantically in search of happiness, whether by means of relationships or fame or money or success, the brass ring on this merry-go-round is simply happiness. They work tirelessly to achieve success or make money, with their noses to the grindstone. All the while happiness is tapping them on the shoulder, but they wave it off because they are trying to succeed or make money in order to find happiness. Their unwillingness to just let the happiness happen is lost in their search for happiness. Pretty mixed up! But it begs the question, would you be willing to give up the hunt for happiness in order to be happy? In order to be happy, you have to be happy. That's it! Without the judgments about whether you deserve to be happy or not. It's just a choice.

If you could choose anything, what would you choose; what do you truly desire to create? What would your life be like if you were to invent yourself and create yourself, moment by moment? All that would be required is your willingness to let go of the definitions and decisions you created that limit what you would or would not do to create what you desire. For you to see and choose different possibilities than you have ever chosen before, you have to shift your attitude. You've got to be willing to do whatever it takes to get where you truly wish to be, including being happy.

People say, "I want to have lots of money." And I ask them, "Okay. Are you willing to be or do whatever it takes?" "Well, everything except hurting somebody. Everything except walking over dead people. Everything except…"

"So, you're not willing to do *whatever* it takes to get money."

"You mean I'd *have* to do that?"

"No. But if you are willing to do whatever it takes to get the money, then the vast majority of the time you will never have to do that. But because you're willing to, the universe will start shifting to make your life a different reality."

It is a matter of being rather than doing.

These are questions you have to function from: What can I be and do that is different which would create a different reality? What would I have to be or do to change this in totality?

Notice any judgments that come up for you around all of this. Are you willing to be or do *whatever* it takes? The only reason you can't change something is because there's something you're not willing to be or something you're not willing to do. Isn't that great?

Realize that when you come to the judgment of what you won't do, you come to the conclusion that the only options you have are bound up in this conclusion. However, when you are willing to do anything, the universe shifts everything around and you don't always *have* to do everything. You just have to be *willing*.

What would it take to get a ton of money? What would you have to be or do to make that a reality? People who want a ton of money frequently tell me, "But I'd have to work so hard to get it!"

Well, if you really desired something, wouldn't you work that hard? I would. I'm willing to do whatever it takes to get what I want in life. Are you? The creation of your life is up to *you*. You have to realize that you cannot make anybody else do anything. You can only demand of yourself that you make whatever change you need to make in order to get what you want in life. When you make the demand of you to create, the universe will have your back.

Demand is total allowance. It is the choice you make to create without any points of view or judgments. You are the only one who can choose to keep holding onto, or to let go of, all the judgments and points of view you have used to limit your creations. Ask yourself, "What do I really desire to

51

create here?" You may discover that what you desire to create is not what you would expect.

Realize that if you're not getting what you say you want, it's because you don't truly want it. Stop pretending that this or that is what you want and allow yourself to look at what you are actually creating. For example, I was talking with a woman about how she just doesn't know whether she can stay married to her husband. I asked her what was going on, and she said, "What it boils down to is he grew up with money, invested it really badly, and lost everything. And now he thinks that something should be given to him." Perhaps because her husband came from a privileged class, he believes he is supposed to have money. Therefore, he doesn't understand why people don't give it to him. He's not willing to do whatever it takes to create it.

It turned out that this man was also involved with Access Consciousness®. In fact, after my conversation with his wife, he sent me an email saying he was going back to school and doing other things to get his financial life back on track. And I thought, "Wow, that's so cool that he's found something that he likes."

A month or so later, another participant who knew the man asked why I hadn't hired him.

"What!?" I was shocked. The email he sent me did not say, "I need a job. Can you help me?" He hadn't said, "Would you be interested in hiring me?" He hadn't said anything that sounded like he needed a job. Clearly, he wasn't willing to do what it takes to get a job. He still just expected the universe to provide it for him, and for everybody to be happy with him no matter what, even if he does nothing. That's not a good place to come from.

You have to be willing to make the demand of yourself that, no matter what it takes, you're going to succeed. No matter what it takes, you're going to get money. No matter what you have to do, you're going to get this. When you function from that point of view, the universe does everything it can to contribute to you. That is being in allowance of your needs.

The universe is in allowance of your demand. To be clear, what I am speaking about here is *the demand you make of yourself.* When you make a demand of you, you will have it. You will get it. Demand, as I am presenting it here, does not have the energy of force in it. Force is directed at the desired object or condition; demand of yourself is what creates the desire that will ultimately be fulfilled by the universe's support of you.

If you could have anything you wanted in life, what demands would you make of yourself to get that? Would you be willing to practice "interesting point of view, I have this point of view" with all of the points of view you are using to create the judgments you are choosing? How much of your reality are you creating based on the judgments you are buying as real; the judgments that are the lies that keep you from having everything you desire?

Now, why would you not want to have everything you desire? Did you go blank when I asked that question? Many people do. Do you ever think about getting everything you desire, or do you only think about what you aren't going to get? For so many of us, the idea of what we *aren't* going to get is more real to us than what we *are* going to get.

Allow yourself to look at this and make a shift. Rather than automatically going to "I can't get this," ask yourself, "How can I get this?" and be willing to do or be whatever it takes to have that as your reality.

Most people are not willing to do what it takes to get exactly what they desire. They would like somebody to hand it to them. Some will even repeat the Access Consciousness mantra, "All of life comes to me with ease and joy and glory®" 800 times a day. But they won't leave their house.

When my daughter, Shannon, first started facilitating Access classes, she said to me, "I'm not making any money. What do I do to change that?"

I asked her, "What are you doing now?"

"Well, I'm saying 10 times in the morning and 10 times in the evening, *all of life comes to me with ease and joy and glory.*"

I responded that this is a doing reality in which we all have to do something to get money. I gave her an example that's a bit shocking: If you're a prostitute, you either have to put on a really short skirt and stand on a corner, or you have to put a red light over your door. "Have you done that?" I asked.

Of course, she was taken aback and told me she didn't want to be a prostitute. I said, "I know. But what would be the equivalent of showing people that you have something to offer, actions that you can take to create the life you desire right away?"

Ask yourself if your life would be any different if you were willing to function from this mindset: "You know what? This is what I would like in my life, and I don't care what it takes to get there. I'm *going* to get there."

You've got to ask and discover; how do I get what I want? What do I have to be or do differently to get everything I desire in life?

Do you feel the difference in that energy?

CHAPTER 6:

Will You Ever Have Problems if You Choose to Be in Allowance?

A n interesting point of view some people have is: "When you have allowance, nothing should ever be difficult. Nothing should ever be a problem. Your whole life should be ease, joy, and glory without any pain or suffering." But remember, total allowance includes everything— judgment, difficulty, sorrow, sadness...*everything*; when you are in total allowance, you will *experience everything, and judge nothing*.

Awareness is part of experiencing allowance. Awareness means that you are able to perceive things with only subtle clues. Can you tell if your spouse is angry or sad? Probably. How? "Well, I'm not sure, but it's like I can feel it, even if nothing is said." You probably perceive the anger because it is an important part of your life, as happiness would be. You pick up little hints, where others don't see them. People used to call awareness a mother's intuition when she could tell that her child wasn't feeling well or was getting into trouble in the next room when there was no noise to get her attention. These examples of awareness are what run counter to the beliefs of people who might not be as aware; they will probably be judged as hogwash and laughed off or renamed as something more palatable, like instincts or women's intuition. An interesting point of view.

Allowance, on the other hand, is the process whereby we can rid ourselves of judgments and fixed points of view by the use of "interesting point of view." When you are in allowance, it means that your awareness is running and will detect judgments and points of view, bringing them to your attention. Allowance is the place where we eliminate our newly found judgments by the use of interesting point of view. There are always judgments and fixed points of view flying around on this planet. People are addicted to the idea that there will always be good and bad, right and wrong wherever there are people. Typically, good means that people are aligning with the same point of view, and bad means they are resisting or reacting to it. Many social organizations are based on this idea. The members get together and make sure that only the deserving and right can belong to the organization and the wrong are labeled as bad and excluded. We are great because we are us. You are not with us, so you're against us.

Taking the point of view that when you have allowance, your whole life should be nothing but ease, you have judged what it will mean if you get to that level of allowance. In effect, you have turned allowance into a judgment, a measure of performance if you will. When that happens, it is no longer allowance, but part of a system of judgments. As a result, if you don't have perfect ease – which you judged to be the result of having total allowance – then you assume a wrongness in you and that you don't have total allowance. Allowance means ease; "I'm ill at ease, therefore I'm not in allowance." Instead of turning allowance into a measure of judgment, you might ask the question: "Am I gaining more awareness and more allowance here?"

If you would like to receive from everything, ask to be aware of all your judgments, even the judgments you have about what allowance is. Those are the judgments that we use to *prove* we have allowance for ourselves; however, *proving* we have allowance doesn't work. It's not a contest where we get a medal for being the person voted most in allowance. Proving what's right about us keeps us creating limitation and never engaging in joyful creation.

Try to think about how everything that occurs expands your awareness of what is actually possible. Each person and situation that you come into contact with gives you greater awareness. If you look at the challenging situations of your life through the lens of judgment, you may define them as problems rather than as a way for you to get a level of awareness that you may not have gotten any other way. Again, what if there was nothing right or wrong about what you choose? What if you could receive even greater awareness and possibilities from everything?

If you hit a financial bump or you get ill or lose your job, it is probably not the result of falling out of allowance. This stuff happens on this planet. Being in allowance would be to address your reactions to the loss of health or job through interesting point of view. What are the emotions and self-recriminations that people go through when they get fired? It can be devastating. Lying awake at night wondering where you went wrong and what's wrong with you doesn't do much to find you a job. So, it's an interesting point of view that I think

I lost my job because there is something wrong with me. It's an interesting point of view that I have this point of view. You lay in bed in allowance and things begin to change. When you practice interesting point of view, you change the energy of your sorrow and loss, and you feel ease creeping back into you. Then, you can start asking questions geared for what you desire. "What would it take for me to find a job that would bring me joy and a lot of money? What could I do or be to bring this about?"

Here's where allowance and awareness come together. Awareness gives you a direction or a hint about something you had never thought of. You pull it into your mind and give it some thought, but old training steps in. The judgment tells you that you'll always be a loser so what's the use? What seems at first to be promising begins to lose its allure and you go back to being hopelessly unemployed. In comes interesting point of view – the piece that challenges those very kinds of judgment. The energy changes and the hints by your awareness become a real possibility.

The answer to the question asked in the title of this chapter is a resounding yes! You will have problems, even if you are fully in allowance. Allowance doesn't make you a robot; you are a real person living on a planet full of the best and the worst. Allowance doesn't choose one or the other for you. It simply combats fixed points of view and judgments. A man closed an address to a graduating class with the advice: "Don't pray for fewer problems, pray for more skill." That's what allowance is about. There'll always be problems, but they don't have to lay you low if you maintain yourself in allowance. Allowance includes everything, even joy, peace, abundance and ease. You can't wish the problems of the world away, but you can use allowance as the tool to disarm the energy that comes at you with the judgments.

It is the judgments of right and wrong that lock us up and send us into a tailspin. Every bit of the tangled journey through right and wrong keeps you from creating, because you always have to justify your choices. If you had total allowance, you'd have the freedom to create. For example, start by asking yourself, "What could I choose and be that would allow me to have way more fun than I've ever been willing to have?" Many people think it's stupid to have fun and smart to suffer. This is just crazy stuff!

Do you see that you've got to really look at your points of view and all that they create? *You* are the one who can choose to have fun with what you create. *You* are the one who can choose to suffer. The situations that you create in your life may not always be easy, but you can ask for as much ease as possible with all of them. And when you choose to be in allowance, you keep your eyes open, and your awareness engaged to assist you as you walk along the path of your life.

CHAPTER 7:

Allowance Is Not Being a Doormat

I t would be wonderful if someone in allowance would be given a placard to wear on their back which would read: "Be kind to me; I'm in allowance." Of course, no one would do that, but sometimes, when first practicing allowance, people expect it. The truth is, whether or not you are in allowance, people will tend to treat you as they always have. Some will try to control you through anger, shame, or manipulation. Because you are in allowance doesn't change anyone's point of view but yours. So, if you are still treated like that, what can you do and still maintain your allowance?

Two businessmen walk by a sidewalk news stand and one of them, who practices allowance, picks up a paper. As he reaches for his wallet, the vendor says: "It must be tough. Here it is, nine o'clock in the morning and you two are strolling along your way to work to your shiny office, wearing your five hundred-dollar suits. The rest of us in the world have to really work for a living while you guys sit up in a tower looking down at us, like vultures on a telephone pole, just waiting for a chance to take our money!"

The man pulls out the money for the paper, drops a tip in the tip jar and turns to walk on with his friend.

The friend says: "That guy is a jerk! Why do you do business with him, anyway?"

The man answers: "His opinions and judgments are simply an interesting point of view. I don't buy them. However, he is in a convenient location on the way to the office."

"But he's so rude!"

"Why would I allow a rude jerk like that guy to tell me where to buy a paper?"

The word allowance may bring to mind allowing others to run over you at will. When discussing allowance with some parents, the question was asked, "Are you telling me that I have to let my kids do anything they want? My house would be in ruins!" This is a good time to mention that allowance is NOT laissez-faire! It's not forgiving. It's not being nice. It is simply a tool you can use to get out of the clutches of unwanted points of view and judgments. Nothing is said about being a doormat or being unable to stand up for yourself. Just do it without judging.

If you have ever had an assertiveness training course, you might remember the difference between assertiveness and aggressiveness. When people are aggressive, they broadcast enormous energy to control others or gain power over them. Assertiveness involves recognizing the energy of a situation and simply allowing it to pass on by, leaving the assertive person untouched. Assertiveness might fit with allowance, while aggression might be judgment, toxic points of view and all the energy that they broadcast. While allowance does mean allowing people to have their points of view, it is also a tool for you to avoid *buying* their points of view, thereby not being controlled by their energy. The newspaper seller is trying to make the businessman feel guilty, because of the disparity in their financial conditions. Should the businessman get a sinking feeling in his stomach at the conversation, he likely bought the judgment of the newspaper man. Buying a judgment will often reveal itself as a feeling or sensation. It also means that he already had the seeds of that judgment within himself but was unaware.

A judgment is a means of directing energy at a person that locks up or solidifies a fixed point of view. The jibe about the five-hundred-dollar suit makes the point of view that it is wrong for him to have a lot of money. If he buys this judgment, it solidifies and grows, and might direct him to do things to limit his own income, so that he can be true to the judgment. When we use "interesting point of view" in allowance, the energy of the judgment does not cling to us, but goes right on by, leaving us unscathed. We can buy a newspaper where we choose.

Attempts to control us often turn our own fixed points of view and the judgments that we've already bought against us. If a person carries guilt about not doing things right, simply calling out a mistake will engage all of the fixed points of view surrounding that judgment, and not doing things right will become a self-fulfilling prophecy. This is where doing a "judgment housecleaning" becomes important. If you turned your self-judgments and the fixed points of view about yourself into "interesting points of view," there is nothing for the controller to get a hold of, and you can remain who you actually are, not what the other person is trying to make you into.

Sitting in the break room with the rest of the staff, reading a report you're working on, your boss storms in with a red face, anger written all over him. "You're so damned slow, I'd have to drive a stake into the ground just to see if you were moving! Let's go! You need to get those reports done by tomorrow. I don't care if you have to stay here and work all night!"

Interestingly, you know that the reports need to be done. In fact, you've only got a few remaining to be finished, and your boss knows that you are nearly done. So why all the put-downs and yelling? That's a good question. Does his behavior have anything to do with the reports? With your performance? Probably not. It does, however, have a lot to do with controlling you.

You have some choices at this point. You can shrink with embarrassment at having been taken down by your boss, or you can become angry and, after he leaves, go on a rampage yourself, informing everyone about what an arrogant, mean-spirited rat the boss is. You can follow after the boss and confront him by telling him what a jerk he is. There is nothing right or wrong about any of these responses; however, there are things to be considered here. What judgments of yourself did your boss's rant bring to the surface? A belief in your own ineptitude? Weakness? Shame from some past experience? A fixed point of view that all bosses are power hungry? How easy would it be to control you simply by hitting one of these "reaction buttons"? You might want to run them through some allowance. "What buttons did he hit that made me react?" Discovering what they might have been, you can do "interesting point of view that I bought these judgments."

On the other hand, you can be in allowance. If you choose to be in allowance, you are able to take the initial accusation for what it is, an interesting point of view, and go back to reading your report and sipping coffee. Or you can get up and face your boss and, rather than confront him from a position of defensiveness brought about by his attempt to control you, you can use your awareness and let him know that treating you in that fashion won't work for you. It compares well with using assertiveness instead of aggression. Being in allowance means that you are not judging your boss as good or bad, but you are informing him that his behavior isn't acceptable to you.

Anger is simply directed energy. We all have an infinite amount of energy available to us for a whole variety of uses, one of which is the expression of anger. It's helpful to understand about anger as a tool for controlling others. There are a several ways to look at anger based on what brought it about. Suppose you are working in the garage and a concrete block falls off of the shelf and lands on your toes. It hurts! A lot! Almost instantly, that hurt turns into anger. You throw whatever you were holding across the room and start swearing a blue streak at the top of your lungs. When we experience pain or intense surprise, it often brings up energy that needs expression. When you hurt your toe and you felt the pain, the energy built up and was released in an instant, driving you to throw things and swear. Are you mad at the concrete block? Of course not! The block doesn't care! What were you angry at? The pain. It's only later that you start blaming yourself or others for leaving the concrete block where it could fall. The anger, though, is simply massive energy, in this case brought on by pain.

Someone with a "short fuse" carries anger right near the surface, so any little stimulus will unleash a tempest. Even the smallest thing can set it off. This is simply a magnification of the sore toe incident. It is still energy that is held in until needed. Like a boil on the skin, it erupts for no visible reason. It just shows up. The same is true for the "short fuse." The "buttons" for setting off a tirade are things like a low frustration tolerance or the point of view that everybody's got something against you. Very often the person with the short fuse won't even know it exists.

Can someone in allowance be angry? Yes! You can confront someone very strongly, right to their face; however, if you are in allowance, you are free to do so without judgment. Interestingly, if you confront a person from a place of allowance, they'll very likely accept the confrontation. It's the energy of judgment and anger that escalate arguments. The definition of allowance is simple; be willing to live your life with its ups and downs, highs and lows, without judgment. Period. No rule book. The reason someone goes through the effort of learning how to be in allowance is to get rid of the rules that are judgment based. When we fall out of allowance, we get to crawl into the black and white limitations of a polar, right and wrong, good and bad existence, where we are not allowed to live entirely by choice. Allowance is a choice; as is falling out of allowance.

Allowance is the perfect tool for dealing with those who would control or hurt you. When someone tries to control you and you are in allowance, you have awareness, interesting point of view, and question to defuse it.

Amazingly, there is no international fellowship of people in allowance. No clubs. No congregations. No associations. There are individuals who practice awareness and eliminate judgments and fixed points of view through the practice of allowance. If you ever went to a get-together of "People in Allowance," a nonexistent group, you would immediately notice that they come in all shapes, colors, sizes, energies, and personalities. Being in allowance does not mean homogeneity; that is the aim of judgments and fixed points of view. People who are not in allowance tend to want everyone to live like their picture of what should and should not be. If you can't or won't do that, there will likely be judgments or possibly anger aimed at you to bring you into line. One definition of allowance is the willingness to experience everything, good and bad, without judgment. Judgment is defined as aligning or agreeing with or resisting or reacting to a point of view.

Passive aggression is a way to express anger with a denial clause attached. The anger is often expressed verbally through cutting remarks or innuendo. A man who has a large nose might be targeted by someone in a group of people telling a joke about a guy with a big nose. Everyone laughs and the joke teller demurs saying: "I didn't mean it; I was just joking." If the man with the large nose reacts in any way, the jokester can then attack him with something like, "Don't be so thin-skinned. Geez! Can't you take a joke?" There is no way that the subject of this jokester can fight back. Except through allowance. It's all just an interesting point of view. The jokester and the joke fired at him? Interesting point of view. Are my feelings hurt? Interesting point of view that I should let a turkey like this guy affect me and hurt me. Once again, the aim of the joke was to cause a reaction. Allowance means no resistance and no reaction. The joke falls flat because the target didn't flinch, and the group turns its negative attention toward the joke and the jokester instead. Allowance is a fantastic way of dealing with jokesters.

Anger can also be expressed by passively manipulating. There are an infinite number of ways in which the manipulation can be used in this manner. For example, a dad tells his son, who is playing games on his phone, to haul out the trash. The son says, "Okay" but doesn't move. In a few minutes, the dad says once again, "Would you please haul out the trash?" "Sure, Dad, I said I would." Another five minutes goes by and finally, the dad has had it! "I told you to haul out the trash! Put down that game or I'll take that phone away and you won't be playing anymore! Now get moving!" The boy gets up slowly and says: "Jeez Dad, you don't have to go ballistic! I told you I'd haul it out! What the heck is wrong with you?" Dad just got smacked with the power of the passive. After the second request, it was no longer hauling the trash that was the issue; it was who has the power.

If people get hooked in by a passive manipulation or passive aggressive behavior, it probably indicates that they have a self-judgment or point of view that acts as a button for the passive person to push, thus leading to a flurry of more judgment.

This could have been done with allowance. "What judgments or points of view have I bought and buried that would cause me to become so defensive and angry?" "What judgments of myself have I created and bought as a result of this encounter? Guilt? I'm a bad father? Interesting point of view that I have those judgments of myself." "What judgments do I have about my son that are precipitating this episode? Children should always obey their parents immediately, and if they don't it means I'm a weak or bad parent?"

Then, he can use "It's an interesting point of view that I feel that he is challenging my power. It's an interesting point of view that I have in me a need to be in control and have power." Then, without judging himself as a bad parent, or a weakling, or as the king of his realm, the dad is able to change the tenor of the discussion, get the trash hauled, and nobody's feathers get ruffled. He might ask the question out loud, "What would it take to have you to do your job and haul the trash right now without a confrontation?" The son's reaction will be considerably different. If he balks, simply repeat the question. The trash will get hauled. Allowance makes a more rational way of dealing with resistant people possible, whether it's your kids, coworkers, or the garbage man. When you are in allowance, when people come at you with challenging points of view, expecting to control you with your reactions, they become disarmed because there is no reaction or resistance on your part. The whole idea was to get a reaction.

Anger, passive or aggressive, amounts to a tug of war over power. The side with the biggest pull wins the contest. But in order for that to take place, both parties have to grab the end of the rope. Someone says: "You're ugly and stupid. My dog is worth more than you!" At this point there is a choice. If you choose allowance, and go into interesting point of view, there is a one-sided tug of war that goes nowhere. He called you a name. Interesting point of view. He's angry. Interesting point of view. If it escalates, you might take more drastic measures, like telling him in no uncertain terms that his behavior isn't going to work for you. Keeping interesting point of view in mind, you might confront the person loudly, "Hey," in your loudest voice. "Dig the dirt out of your ears! I told you that that is not going to work for me!" (Just because you're in allowance doesn't mean that you are not free to project your *own* energy!) Just don't judge either your antagonist or yourself.

On this planet, you will be confronted by people who are rude or selfish or chronically angry, or who display a host of other hurtful behaviors. It is not that you won't be confronted by people's malignant actions; you will. The question is how to deal with them as they arise without buying judgments about either you or them. It requires nothing out of the ordinary, just what you have already developed.

First of all, when you are in allowance, you will be in awareness. You will "notice" things both about your senses and what's happening in the world around you. A teenage girl was asked by a carload of friends to go to a party. She went and there was trouble that ended in a couple of kids being hospitalized and the police hauling the rest of the partygoers down to the police station to either be charged or picked up by their parents. The desk officer asked one girl what she was doing there. "Do you mean that you didn't think anything would happen when this bunch of druggies got together?" She responded that she had a negative feeling about the whole thing, but it sounded so fun, she just brushed it off as being excited and went along. She *had* awareness but ignored it instead of acting on it through allowance and question. "What is this awareness I'm sensing in my belly? Will I have problems if I attend the party? Is my thinking that nothing will happen real?" As it was, though, she did experience something valuable in her journey to the local police department. When you get that special "bellyache" that tells you something bad is going to happen, listen to it! That's what your awareness is for. The best possible way to defend yourself in a threatening situation is to not be there. If everybody around you is giving you a bad time for leaving, that's nothing but a pile of interesting points of view! Get out of there.

Be in allowance and be aware. Don't be a doormat.

CHAPTER 8:

Allowance of Yourself

T otal allowance is just a choice. No matter what you're thinking, doing, or being, you can choose to be in allowance of it. It's all just an interesting point of view.

When I become aware that I'm feeling like I have to be right about something, I say to myself, "Interesting point of view, I think I have to be right." I don't ever really *have* to be right. Remember, rightness is a judgment that nearly always needs to be defended, putting you out of allowance. It is not a very useful practice. I don't have to be right; I just have to be aware.

Suppose you crawl up a ladder to the highest part of a tree, saw in hand, to take down a dead limb. It's a little scary, but you do it anyway because it's something of an adventure and it feels kind of good to show off for the neighbors. Your next-door neighbor leans over the fence and asks if you'd like him to hold the ladder, to which you respond, "No, I'm doing fine." Inside, though, you're feeling a bit shaky. In fact, you're a bit scared, but with the neighbor watching, you won't let on that you are. Finally, the branch drops causing the tree and the ladder to shake, so you hang on to the ladder tighter. When the shaking of the tree, not your knees, which continue to shake, stops, you slowly climb down.

You might ask yourself, "What judgments or points of view did I use to make myself climb up there and do that?"

Acknowledge where you are, and you can choose to change. You've got to see when you're choosing and what your choice is. And be in allowance of your choice—not come to conclusion about whether it's right or wrong or good or bad (or if your neighbor will think less of you.)

In class, I suggested that a participant go through every point of view she had every morning and repeat, "Interesting point of view, I have this point of view." After just a few days, she saw that for every point of view she had, she also had points of view that were counter to it. By having disparate points of view, she was able to keep herself in a constant state of conflict while thinking that somehow, she was getting better. It wasn't until she began to use the tool, "interesting point of view," that she realized how many varied points of view she was holding onto.

Once she began this practice, she was able to receive more awareness of what her points of view were. And from that space, she began to unravel the unconsciousness she had been functioning from. Her choice to receive this awareness made all the difference. Without her choice, she would not have gained the clarity that she required to make the changes she desired.

It is important to recognize that you cannot give anyone anything they can't receive. They simply won't have it! And if you attempt to give someone more than they can receive, they will return it to you with daggers attached. You have to be in allowance of what people can receive. And "people" includes you! How much are you willing to receive?

Many of us already know that we're fully able to receive total judgment at any time...and believe it. *That* we'll believe in a heartbeat. The process for receiving judgment is the same as the process for receiving what you truly desire. It is as easy to eat filet mignon as it is to eat burned walrus liver, so why choose the charred, greasy liver? What stands in your way?

Many people believe they cannot change things they haven't yet changed. Is that a point of view or a judgment? If you stand back and look at this notion,

77

it is easy to see the absurdity of it. Just because you have not *yet* changed something doesn't mean you can't change it. It just means that, so far, you have not done whatever it takes to change it.

When we choose to be in allowance, we begin to free ourselves from the judgments that we have been using to limit ourselves, whether those judgments are ours or anyone else's. Allowance gives us the keys to being everything we truly can be, whereas every time we make a judgment of ourselves real, we are struggling against being who we truly are. Everything we've decided we don't like about ourselves is the thing about us that is *really* us, but that we don't want to see.

Our self-judgment always makes it wrong to be what we've decided we already are that we're not supposed to be. You might have heard of no-fault insurance? This is different. This is the MY-fault insurance plan. If it's me, it's wrong. Within that judgment lies the unwillingness to be in allowance of everything—where you can be a dictator, or a jerk, or bold, or aggressive, or too much, or whatever. Sometimes you're too much. By whose judgment?

I believe that people only accuse us of what they, themselves, are doing. So, when someone accuses you of something, they are letting you know a part of how they judge themselves. If someone accuses you or belittles you, and you go to a place of "I don't like it that you say that about me," you are making their judgment about *you*, that is to say, buying it at face value, and not acknowledging that it is actually about *them*. Not only are you making it personal, but you're also making it *real* rather than realizing it's an invention. It leads you to see yourself as diminished instead of as the infinite being you really are. There is nothing at all real about an accusation. It simply alerts our awareness that the person has problems they're trying hand to you. But many of us will choose react to the accusation, simply because we are in the habit of being accused, by ourselves and others. When will you gain allowance for all the things you judge about yourself? Here's a suggestion: write down a list of all the things you think are the worst things about you, then write down all the things you think are the best things about you. Look at both lists and ask, "What judgments do I have to have to keep these points of view in existence?" Because it is guaranteed that both the "best" and "worst" things are based on judgments you have that you haven't yet acknowledged.

Instead, you can have allowance. Then you won't have to judge what's best for you or anyone else. You can simply say, "Okay, this is what I am." If someone doesn't like what you have chosen, that could be filed under "interesting point of view"!

With this exercise you can start to uncover what is really true about you that you don't want to see –

and certainly don't want anybody else to see. Once you're willing to see anything about yourself that you have decided is not something other people can or should see, then *you'll* not only be able to see it, but rid yourself of it by recognizing that it's an interesting point of view. When you recognize that the things you become aware of were the result of your own choices, you can change them. But first you have to claim, own, and acknowledge them. You have to go, "Okay. I'm a jerk; that's not who I want to be!"

Be in allowance of wherever you are in life. Use your awareness and choose to create from what is… not what you think should be or shouldn't be. And if there is something you truly would like to change, simply ask yourself, "What would I have to be or do to change this in totality?"

CHAPTER 9:

Choose to Be You

Allowance of yourself is knowing that you're going to be everything you are whether anybody likes it or not! I don't care if people like me. I don't care if people follow me. I don't care if people think I'm an asshole. None of that matters to me. My point of view is that everything is an interesting point of view. And I am always looking for what else is possible.

One day I had lunch with the mayor of the region in Italy where we bought a castle. This castle was built in the 900s and had been uninhabited and neglected for the past 20 years. Recently, we have turned the castle into a place where people can come to experience the nurturing for their bodies and beings that is possible with true elegance. But originally, at the time of my lunch with the mayor, we were looking to turn the castle into a boutique hotel. This particular lunch was planned in order to discuss the logistics of the castle becoming a hotel.

The mayor started telling me how I needed to do things for him in order to get the necessary permit. My point of view was, "Look, aren't we going to create more income for this village than they've had in years? And they are trying to stop me? Okay, good. So I will not ask for a conditional use permit to turn the venue into a hotel. Instead, I will turn it into a private club. Then, I don't need anyone's permission. Now, is that allowance? Yes. That is allowance of his fixed point of view, and that I am the valuable product. How often do you allow yourself to be the valuable product?

Being the valuable product is knowing that you know what's true and you know what you will do and you know what you will be to create the greatest for everybody, including you. It is honoring and valuing yourself. If you're not in allowance of yourself and you don't value yourself, then you always try to understand other people's points of view as though their awareness is greater than yours. What would happen if you were to ask, "What awareness do I have here that I'm not willing to have?"

Allowance is knowing that you're having an awareness and not putting it in context with other people. With the castle, the moment I first saw it, I knew what it could become. At that time, I could see what it has turned into today. And I knew that it would contribute to the people living in that village, bringing in money, jobs, and possibilities. I had the awareness of all of that and was willing to know what I know regardless of what anyone else determined would be right or wrong from their point of view.

Not putting your awareness into context with other people eliminates the insanity people create with their need to be validated. In my opinion, validation is a crock of shit that people use to pretend that they are finally getting somewhere. There is only one person in the world who can actually validate you, and that is you. And that is only done by being in total allowance of yourself, acknowledging what is true for you, and not bowing down and giving up or giving in. Be aware of all of that and ask yourself, "What am I really trying to do?" Instead of looking for the power of you, look for the allowance of you, without a point of view.

If you have no point of view about you, you get to be anything. When you can be anything, you can do anything. When you can do anything, you can have anything. When you can have anything, you can create anything. When you can create anything, you can create a different world.

CHAPTER 10:

Judgment Is Not Caring

A woman who attended a class on allowance shared that, in her point of view, she can create only when she is *not* in allowance of herself. Part of that point of view was, if she were to be in allowance of herself, she would be so complacent that she wouldn't create anything of value, and that she would waste her life and do nothing.

Does being in allowance actually make a person complacent? It's not that a person can't be complacent, but to be so is really a choice that doesn't have much to do with allowance. There was also a judgment that she would remain complacent unless she was judged into action. She seemed to be saying that the judgments in her life were the only things that spurred her to act. Really? The same theme applies to her point of view that she would waste her life and do nothing if she weren't prodded by other people's judgments and point of view.

Using the judgments implied in the term "wasting her life" to drive her seemed to be her way of not making a choice. She would rather be a slave to those judgments than to choose the life she would really like. But what if she were in allowance of wasting her life? Would that possibly lead to a different choice? So many people think that you have to *do* something in order to create your life. Yes, there are certain actions that are required to bring your creations into being, but creation is not about doing; creation is about being. "What can I be that would bring this to pass?" is a broad picture. "What can I do?" is a much smaller picture, like going from task to task.

In Access Consciousness we look at you from the point of view that you are an infinite being. An infinite being has the ability to perceive, to know, to be, and to receive *infinitely*. You can choose to function as an infinite being and let go of the limitations that keep you from your ability to perceive, know, be, and receive anything and everything. Or you can choose to function as a finite being and hold onto the judgments and points of view that keep your world a tiny place, full of rightness and wrongness. What would you like to choose?

When it comes to functioning as an infinite being, one interesting point of view that often shows up is: "If I were an infinite being, I'd do nothing. I'd just be." What? No, if you were an infinite being, you'd do *everything*! Imagine being given the freedom to do and be what you wish to do or be, with no punitive, authoritative points of view holding you down. Infinite beings don't sit around and wait; they create! When asked if she enjoyed doing nothing, the woman said that when she does nothing, she judges herself. There are, after all, a great many rules, commandments, points of view and judgments about the idle hand being the devil's workshop. If she doesn't judge herself along those lines, there will be plenty of others willing to judge her as well.

She asked if she should just be in allowance of wasting her life for a while. "Should I be in allowance of…" is the equivalent of asking permission to be in allowance. Who would she ask that of? The second she asked, she judged that she was no longer the person running her life and it would be someone else's doing if things went amiss. Clearly, she was *not* in allowance of the fact that she could choose to do nothing if she wanted to. Instead, she wanted to come to a conclusion about what she was judging. She was trying to decide what she "should" do, which is a conclusion. There is no should with allowance. Should is based on right and wrong. With total allowance, there is only choice and what that choice creates. The woman was looking to define the right way to "be" and seeking to apply this conclusion to "doing nothing" to the area of her life that she was judging.

This judgment was stopping her from actually creating. She could stop herself from doing *anything* with that judgment. Instead of recognizing, "Interesting point of view that I can stop myself with my judgments." She was using judgment to stop herself and to force herself to do things. Somewhat like walking down a path that has a concrete barrier on it. She crawls over the barrier with great effort, then turns around and moves it into the path ahead of her so that she can crawl over it again. That may sound crazy, but it is all around us; people creating their own impediments through judgment.

Being in allowance here would be to say, "Interesting point of view, I have this point of view." When I asked her what point of view she was not acknowledging, she responded with the same assertion as before: that she was just wasting her life and not being a contribution.

Her points of view were judgments. Not all points of view are judgments, but these were. She went on to give another example from her life that provided even more clarity about where she was functioning from. She said, "As a mom, if I'm in total allowance of whatever my son chooses, then, after a certain point, I start feeling that I'm uncaring." After having come to the conclusion that she must avoid allowance, she thinks judgment is "caring," which is in accordance with her idea that judgment will prod her to act in an acceptable way. She reasons that this judgment of herself equates to caring about herself. It's not hard to understand why she is unwilling to be in allowance, given what she believes. However, if she were to be in allowance of herself, she could be in allowance of her son and wouldn't think that the judgment is caring. She could simply choose the way that she would like to parent. Perhaps, she would just care for her son, without the fuss.

Do you have the point of view that judgment is caring? Did you, perhaps, learn that from your parents? No matter who you learned it from—even if you learned it from the most holy, anointed person in the world—it doesn't make it true. It doesn't make it real. Judgment is never caring. Caring does not require judgment.

Caring is always the willingness to know what's true for you. It's being willing to choose that regardless of anybody else's point of view. *That* is the place of not having to align and agree or resist and react to any of the energies that anyone is sending your way. This is one purpose of using the "interesting point of view" tool: to take the "charge" off the points of view you are aware of—whether they are yours or anyone else's.

Remember, sometimes you will have a "negative awareness" that might seem like a judgment. For example, say you think that someone you know is lazy. Lazy has a negative connotation to many people. Yet it could be an accurate assessment of where someone is functioning from. You could be in allowance of an employee who exhibits laziness on the job without judging the value of that as good or bad. You can then choose a course of action if you deem that he is creating a problem for you. "Negative awareness" does not have the charge of right or wrong that comes with a judgment. When in allowance, you won't be projecting the energy of judgment, so this employee won't react as if you were. This is a whole new dynamic.

If you're ever uncertain whether you are having a negative awareness or a judgment, look at it and go, "Interesting point of view I have the point of view about this being a negative awareness." And then, "Interesting point of view I have the point of view that this is a judgment." If you do interesting point of view, eventually you'll get clear about which one it is. But you've got to start with "interesting point of view, I have this point of view."

Remember, every point of view is just an interesting point of view. Free yourself from any fixation you have on the rightness or wrongness of your points of view. Allow yourself to have the awareness from which you can choose whatever will create the life and world you truly desire. Ask yourself, "What can I be that would create even more than I can imagine?" The only one who can truly stop you is you. And you would choose that for what reason? There are different possibilities available for you. What possible caring can you truly choose now?

Try imagining being whatever you have decided you will not be and clear any of the stuck energies that come up around that. Look at what energy, space, consciousness, and choice you can be to be the vicious, evil demon from hell you truly be. The whole purpose of this is to get people out of the judgments they may have about being a vicious demon from hell. If you are morbidly afraid of being something, there is a good chance that you have already judged yourself guilty and try to hide the fact from yourself. Looking at it without judgment will allow you to sweep it away as the invention it really is.

It is not uncommon for us to want to be seen as nice people. People are constantly trying to prove that they are nice. When you're trying to prove that you're nice, it's generally because somewhere you have the point of view that you are not. So, facing the points of view you have about that, moving out of the judgment of the wrongness of that, and being willing to be the demon from hell, *if you choose to*, begins to open up different possibilities you may never have considered.

It's all in what you do with it. Intensity, like fire, can be a wonderful thing or a destructive thing. In fact, spending time with someone who is extremely intense can feel like sitting near a woodstove. It can also stimulate you and get you moving. Intensity is a measure of the degree of energy attached to a behavior. We hate with intensity; we love with intensity. We work with intensity; we play with intensity. Intensity is not the activity, love, work, or play; it is the energy with which it is practiced.

People will often look at someone who is pursuing an activity with intensity and get the point of view that it is the activity that is intense, when it's the person engaged in the activity that is intense. Sometimes intense people can be hard to take because everything is set to the highest volume, and it can be overwhelming.

A woman was seeking some guidance on the subject of intensity. She said she was looking for greater ease with her willingness to be the intensity that she saw in a very intense person she knew. What she hadn't thought of was that he could be that intense because he was in allowance of his intensity. To him, it was just an interesting point of view that he was intense, like being tall or short, while she was stuck on what it means to her to be intense. Her point of view was that "intensity" means you have to be self-centered, unfeeling, arrogant, and driven, and she was not willing to be in allowance of it, because she had judgments about being all of those things. She also mentioned that she had a desire to be nice and kind, so she was willing to be intensely kind but not intense in other ways. This is because she had the judgment that all other intensity was a judgable offense.

I asked if other people had told her that she was way too intense, she said, "Yes!" intensely…because she *is* really intense! Whether the woman thought that she was different and off-putting to other people or something else, she came to the belief that her intensity was her enemy. She had great difficulty, in her mind, taking the risk of being in allowance of her nemesis, intensity, fearing that to do so would simply be opening Pandora's Box. So, she tried to find ways of diminishing her intensity so that people would like her, so she could fit in, so she wouldn't explode on people. She was asking to change her habit of not being allowance of her intensity, but she didn't know what that change would look like.

The thing is it doesn't matter *what* it looks like. What matters is being willing to be whatever that intensity is *regardless of what it looks like*. And you've got to ask and have the sense of what really is possible that you haven't considered. It's just a different reality from which you can choose.

And it's all just a choice! So often people their think choices are right or wrong or good or bad. That's judgment, not choice. Would you be willing to let go of everywhere you are not in allowance of the choices you make? Instead of defining what is right or wrong about you, what if you were to choose what actually works for you? What if you could choose to be *everything* that you truly *are* and everything that it is possible for you to be?

CHAPTER 11:

What Are You Creating?

You might recall that most people live lives that are defined by the judgments that they have bought about themselves and their world. You might be one of the people who wanted more than running around a maze like a lab rat, so you began to shed those judgments in order to reveal the "real you." The real you is free of judgment and filled with possibilities that, like fruit hanging from a vine, are yours for the choosing.

We usually think of choice in the same way we think of "decision," which is to say we pick one of two possibilities. Decide! Yes or no. Choice is about "Here's the universe. Choose something and, if you don't like it, choose something else." It's a bit like buying shoes: if you don't like the red ones, put them back and try the brown ones. The difference between these ideas is the difference between being in the box created by judgment and the unbounded choice engendered by awareness.

"I've got a 'green thumb'. Growing healthy plants is really easy for me." "Operating machinery just comes naturally to me." "Accounting and numbers are not only easy for me, but I love working with figures. The tougher the problem, the more fun it is!"

Is there such a thing as a green thumb, a mechanical marvel, or a math genius? Probably not. A better question might be, "How much will I allow myself to be?" or "How much can I choose from the font of infinite possibility?" The problem behind living a limited life is not that there are too few choices, it is that people have been taught that choosing is difficult and always carries consequences. People will think you're nice or good if you choose little, but think you are greedy, if you choose a lot. Those judgments seem to be pounded into everybody from childhood on. It's all a mess! The person who has billions is thought to be a greedy Scrooge, even though he or she lavishes a fortune on people who are not as wealthy. It's almost like a conspiracy to prevent a person from becoming all they can be and creating an unlimited life filled with possibility. If you have any of these prejudices, you might want to haul out your "interesting point of view" tool and put it to work. A man says, "We're poor, but we're honest," a dig at those wealthier than him. Little does he realize judgment is the very thing that prevents him from having more. It's a justification.

Let's face it; it is easy to get a case of "kid in the candy store" when confronted with infinite choice. It can be overwhelming. If the Halloween candy bag is small, the quantity of candy will be small, even though the people at the door are willing to load it up. If you know what you're looking for, you will probably see people creating ways in which they can avoid choosing the lives that they really desire.

A participant in one of my classes commented that he "copied" other people's creations, thinking that it was a way to create more. Now, why would any of us copy someone else? Could it be that we're unwilling to be the brilliant people we actually are?

What have you done to avoid every single, solitary element of what would create you as being brilliant? What choices can you make to get rid of the self-judgment that keeps you from understanding that you have the capacity to know whatever you wish to know and be whatever you wish to be?

Recognize that when you get fascinated by anybody else's universe you begin to copy and duplicate them, thinking that maybe they have a better universe than you do. The next time you find yourself doing that, ask, "Am I willing to totally exchange worlds with this person? Am I willing to take this person's world and let them have mine?" Be honest. If you discover that you would not be willing to totally swap with this person, why would you be fascinated by their world? Why wouldn't you be fascinated by how amazing your own world is?

Remember, you are the one who is creating your life and world. If there is anything that you would like to change, you can change it. Allowance for whatever you are aware of is key to creating ease with changing any area of your life. You have to let yourself look at where you are functioning in the present.

Do you believe other people are smarter than you? If you are willing to look at somebody else's point of view and have more allowance for theirs than yours, it is because you are not actually willing to see yours.

You've got to look at all of this...not from the wrongness of anything but from the point of view of what's actually going to create the most in your life. Looking at what it is you are actually creating can sometimes require that you let go of the stories you have been telling yourself.

For example, a class participant told me that he had not been using his potency due to a fear of creating conflict. I asked him what he loved about creating conflict. As you may imagine, this was not the direction he expected our conversation to go.

He had not asked himself the question of what he *loved* about creating conflict. The story he was telling himself was that he was avoiding conflict and that it had to do with his parents' separation. He went on to ask what he could use conflict for.

You see, conflict is always a creation. It is never real. It is never the only possibility in any situation. When I asked him what he loved about creating conflict, he knew right away. It made him feel like he was in charge, and it put him in control. He enjoyed fighting everything and everyone. Yet he was in resistance to that. His resistance to the fact that he liked fighting everything and everyone did not allow him to see all that his fighting was creating.

To be clear, fighting everyone is not bad or good. It simply may not be the best choice available. Or it might. From a space of allowance, he could see what it was that he was actually being and choosing and all that was creating.

To begin to shift his point of view around fighting, I suggested he ask himself the simple question, "I'm fighting this for what reason?" Somewhere he had decided that he loved fighting everything and everyone. If he were to use the tool of interesting point of view, he could say, "Wow! I love fighting everyone and everything! Is that my best choice? Maybe not. Okay, I'll choose something different."

Interesting point of view takes you out of the attachment to your points of view and opens up different choices. As long as that class participant was holding on to the point of view that he loved fighting everything and everyone, he could not choose something different. Choice is one of your greatest superpowers. Your choices create the life you are living.

With this particular man, his choice to fight everything and everyone meant he could not have the expansive and magnificent life he actually wanted to have. To him it was more important to be right than to be free. By fighting everything and everyone, he could know what he was doing all the time and why he was doing it. If he were to give that up, he would have to choose something that would actually create his life. As long as he didn't give up his point of view about fighting, he didn't have to create his life.

What are you creating? Sit on your own shoulder and, without judgment, look at your life. Is there any part of what you see that you don't like? You created it. Is there anything that you really like? You created it. When you come out of your unreal world of judgment and point of view, you are free to create what you really desire with ease, because you won't be fighting yourself. Go ahead and create. You don't need permission; just do it for fun.

Chapter 12:

What Grand and Glorious Adventures Can You Have?

A llowance is recognizing that you cannot control anyone else. Controlling people, including yourself, means creating a picture that you judge to be acceptable, then trying to fit them into it. When I try to control myself, it means that I have a picture or a point of view about myself that I have determined to be good or right; then trying to force myself to conform to that ideal. Next time you have a cold, try to control your nose to stop running and see how it works. The harder you try to control things, the harder they push back.

Allowance is recognizing that when you judge yourself, you cease to exist. You become lost in a sea of other people's points of view about your world. Allowance is the recognition that if you allow yourself to be who you are, without a point of view, you can create yourself as anything you choose. You are allowed to choose what you'd like to have in your life, great or small.

Allowance is recognizing you cannot control anyone else; all you can do is control yourself.

Here's an example:

In 1970, I went to Europe for 6 months by myself. I bought a car and traveled around the continent. In many places, there would be people with signs saying, "Going to [so-and-so place]." So I would pick them up and we'd go wherever their sign said. Because these people were willing to pay me for a ride to the place they wanted to go, I didn't have to worry about expenses while exploring. And I didn't really care where I was going; I was willing to go anywhere.

I discovered something over those 6 months.

Before I left California, I had spent my life being known as my mother's child and my father's child. Then, when I got out on my own, I became my job and my car's owner and my dog's owner. I realized that everybody had put me into the category of where they thought I would belong in their world.

When I was in Europe, however, I didn't belong anywhere. I was just me and I got to invent me anew every day.

I see so few people allowing themselves to reinvent themselves on a daily basis. On a moment-by-moment basis. Who you were 10 seconds ago? Are you still that person?

No, that person is now in the past.

Who are you going to be 10 seconds from now? Do you want to be the same person you are now in the next 10 seconds, or do you want to be in allowance of the fact that you can change? There is a simple way in which you can answer these questions. When you get up in the morning, ask yourself, "Okay, so who am I today and what grand and glorious adventures am I going to have?"

I started practicing this in Europe in 1970. As time went on, I didn't just repeat that reminder every day, I developed an attitude: "Okay, so who am I today and what grand and glorious adventures am I going to have?" And I did have grand and glorious adventures. I took my rides to historic sites that were off the map and met incredible people I would never have met. The trip I took to Europe was so different from what everybody else I knew had taken; it was obvious that I had chosen something different. How it was different didn't really sink in until I returned home.

Once I got back from Europe, I spent hours thinking about just what it was that had changed about me. Finally, it came to me that I was no longer bound by the structures of my past. Instead, I was creating myself in the present for a future that had not yet come to actualization. A whole different possibility exists under those circumstances.

When you go out and meet somebody you're interested in, do you tell them the same stories you've told a hundred times before? If you do, be aware that what you may think is *the same old story* is actually what you keep re-*inventing* as the same story. You are a different person all the time, so how could your story possibly stay the same? The problem is that many of us don't want to change our story. We don't want to know what's really true for us, because if we actually knew what was true for us, then we'd have to admit it to ourselves.

I believe that if you haven't gotten the things you want, you have not been willing to admit what's true for you. The truth is that if you haven't gotten something, it's because you don't really desire it. You may *say* that you desire it, but you have to look at the points of view that you are functioning from to see if that's really the case.

You are the one who chooses which points of view you hold onto and which ones you let go of.

Allowance for you creates the space where you can be vulnerable with your awareness of what you truly desire – not what you think you're *supposed* to desire but what is actually true for you. If you were willing to put aside any judgments of right or wrong, what would you choose?

Very few people allow themselves to begin anew on a daily basis, or on a moment-by-moment basis. Who were you 10 seconds ago? Are you still that person? No, that person is now in the past.

Who are you going to be 10 seconds from now? Do you want to be the same person you are now in the next 10 seconds, or do you want to be in allowance of the fact that you can change? Actually, you change continuously every second, unaware. What if you were aware of yourself? You could become aware by simply asking yourself this question every morning: "Okay, who am I today and what grand and glorious adventures am I going to have?"

The problem is that many of us don't want to change our story. Captain of the football team or the homecoming queen. Being special and never wanting to leave that moment. It's safer, and more comfortable to stay with a story already told; there's less risk of making a mistake and being wrong. But, over time, nobody really cares about our 20-year-old story of fame and glory. Yet, we pattern our lives around that event. We don't want to know what's really true for us because if we actually knew what was true for us, then we'd have to admit that the single incident was not big enough to build a life around. If we leave the fantasy behind us and come into this moment, we start to see the infinite possibilities before us instead of a single event gone by the wayside. And when that awareness happens, we become free to choose whatever makes us happy, like kids in a candy store.

If you haven't gotten the things you want, you probably have not been willing to admit what's true for you, which is to say, let go of the past follies and successes. Here's an example of a man whose story was that he wanted a relationship with someone. He wanted to go "deeper with someone," and still wanted to have sex. But when he went out and met people, what he said he wanted was not showing up. The people that he was attracted to tended to just be interested in sex, not relationships. The reality was that he only wanted sex as well; he just didn't want to acknowledge that fact. When he *did* acknowledge that sex was one of his primary desires, he would immediately go looking for something "beyond that" and "deeper than that," rather than the sex he desired. Wait a minute here! He desired sex and went looking for relationships? When he said he was looking for something more than just sex, he appeared to have been justifying the fact that he just wanted sex, as if sex were somehow wrong if it didn't lead him to a relationship. Were he to just be in allowance of the fact that he was really just interested in sex, then he could start having fun creating himself.

If he would come to acknowledge that he's just in it for the sex and stop judging it by applying the "Is this all there is?" to it, and go into allowance of the entire process, he could stop going in two directions at once. If he could get to the actual acknowledgement of being interested in sex, not relationships, and be in allowance of it, not in judgment of it, not seeing it as a wrongness, whatever else is actually available can finally show up for him.

But until he does come into that allowance, he's always going to be looking for the thing that's out of reach, because he's not actually being present with the thing that's already there. The sex is there; the relationships are not. He's judging the sex and he has nothing. So he can't get anywhere else, because he's not allowing himself to be where he actually is right now.

It is necessary to understand that it is the allowance of you—*precisely as you are in this very moment*—that allows you to acknowledge where you are functioning from. And from that awareness, you can choose to change and create anything, even grand and glorious adventures.

CHAPTER 13:

Allowance and Your Body

I f you are not creating your life, you will not create your body. Yes, that's correct. We do, in fact, create our bodies. This is not a discussion of cleaning up your act by quitting smoking or running a mile every day or lifting weights. This is creating your life from the inside, changing our judgments and points of view of what a body should be and how ours fits into that mold. Have you ever looked at yourself in one of those "bend your body" mirrors at the carnival? Our bodies were designed to function smoothly, but the mirrors of judgment, ours and those of others, warp our view of our bodies and our bodies become what we picture.

Some years ago, I decided that I was getting old enough to step down from the business I founded,

Access Consciousness, and that Dr. Dain Heer, the co-founder of the business, needed to take over. I felt the effects of a long and arduous life on my body, and thought, I might just like to not push it so hard anymore. Although, I kept my hand in as a controlling member of the board.

Now retired, I stopped creating and expanding the business because I was going to set it up for Dain to take it over. When I was functioning from that point of view, nothing moved forward in the business. It was as though the business was trying to retire as well. The people associated with the company deflated a bit and it seemed as if everything had been put on hold.

Then, the board of directors decided that they needed to buy a large space the business was working on in Central America. Suddenly, I had no choice. I needed to add at least another 5 years to my life in order to help complete that project. Soon after, I visited a castle in Italy and realized the business needed to add that to its creations as well. This meant that I would now have to stick around for at least another 10 years. Then some people were hired who ended up creating a mess that I had to untangle. That added another 5 years.

With all of this, I, the unretired owner, would have to stick around for 15 more years. Suddenly, my body stopped being as decrepit and old as it had been previously. Why? Because when you start creating your life, you also start creating your body. I was in allowance of my body—both its aging and its energy and I went back to work. While I may not have been as spry as I used to be, I was in allowance of that. The more I created my life, though, the more my body responded with energy.

A woman asked me about being in allowance when you are not happy with the perception that your body is deteriorating, or that it is aging in a bad way. She could ask herself, "I would choose to have that point of view for what reason?" Think about what you might justify with the point of view that you are deteriorating. For many people, that particular point of view justifies that they are so old that they don't have to create anymore. You have to continuously be asking, "What do I *really* want to create here?" If you are not creating your life, be assured that it will continue to be created, but just not by you.

When it comes to bodies, it is unfortunate that so many people would rather judge their bodies than be in allowance. They actually like judging their bodies, in a way, and they choose that judgment over and over. They physically actualize the points of view they have about their bodies, and then they get upset with their bodies for becoming what they have created.

A good example of this came from a woman in an Allowance class. In response to the suggestion that she actually likes judging her body, she said, "Yes, but I'm sick and tired of it. My body keeps getting ill." Do you see that? With the point of view that she was sick and tired of her body, her body was getting sick and tired!

Rather than fighting against her body to change this, I asked her to look at what judgments she had about her body. Immediately she came up with several, one of which was that her body was too fat. I then suggested that she use the tool of interesting point of view. In this case, "Interesting point of view I have the point of view that my body is too fat." I asked if her body likes being fat, to which she said, "Yes." With this information she could use the tool: "Interesting point of view I have that point of view. Interesting point of view my body has that point of view. Interesting point of view we have that point of view."

So much more is possible than simply judging your body. You see, your body will actually create *with* you. It will show you the points of view you are using to create your life. If you move beyond your conclusions and actually choose to be vulnerable enough to ask a question, doors will open up to possibilities you may never have imagined. You've simply got to ask a question that's open-ended enough to allow the universe to give you even more and greater than you can imagine. Again, your body will show you the points of view you are functioning from. Remember that it is the points of view you have that create your life and world. What points of view do you have about your life? What points of view do you have about your body?

The question has been asked: "How often do I have to do the allowance question thing?" The answer is, "Every time you are aware that you are uttering something about your body or your life." *My feet always hurt.* Whether you think that or say it, it is a point of view and a judgment. It's an interesting point of view that your feet always hurt. Is it true that they *always* hurt? "Interesting, that I have a point of view that my feet always hurt. Interesting point of view that I have that point of view."

The point here is that you learn to listen to yourself talk and think, and when the red flags of judgment and points of view pop up, that's the time to exercise your allowance. Listen and question and allowance.

Total allowance is the willingness to see what you and your body need, to see what's required to create a different possibility. You cannot know what you and your body truly need until you're willing to have total allowance.

same sort of glow also emanates from people who are comfortable in their own bodies and sexualness.

Self-esteem and physical well-being are tied up with our sexual selves. People sometimes forget in the rush to have orgasms that there is much more to sex than that delightful act. This doesn't mean that orgasms aren't an integral part of sex; it is that they are but a part of what sexualness is.

What would happen if sex started happening before the sheets were tossed back? What if the energy of people's sexualness co-mingled and their attraction to one another increased as they gave and received that energy? The increase in that energy might very well increase the sense of well-being each person has with their body and their being, and intensify what happens between the sheets. And they probably aren't even aware that the sex had begun much earlier than their physical encounter.

If the people involved are both aware of themselves, their beingness and their sexualness, there doesn't need to be a lot of the usual "What's a nice person like you doing in a place like this?" sort of pickup line.

There was a man named Ed who was "as ugly as a mud fence," in his own words. If you saw him at a distance, you'd think the guy had lived a life of dissipation, which, years before, was in fact true. His life had been a bad train wreck! However, he eventually made some changes and became comfortable with himself in all ways, including sex. He stuck out in a crowd, not because of his homeliness, but because he radiated energy that was filled with life, and joy, and receptivity. He was receptive to people, and they would flock to him wanting him to pay attention to them.

It was Ed's habit to give blood when the bloodmobile was in town. His idea was that giving blood was something that he could do to help the world that cost him only a little of his time and a pint of his blood. Besides, they provided cookies and lemonade.

When it was his turn to lie on the table, the nurse would begin asking which arm, tell him to roll up his sleeve, and so on. Before she even got the whole monologue out, he said a couple words to her, and they looked one another in the eye. At that point, there was definitely energy, sexual energy, flying around the table. The nurse would find an excuse to reach across him and come into greater contact with him. When she had completed attaching the line and telling him to keep squeezing the tennis ball, she moved on to the next donor, walking straighter and smiling. This has been called "strutting one's stuff," an accurate description in this case. And yet, there was no actual, physical sex. She looked great; he looked younger. In ten minutes of experiencing their sexual being without judgment and deriving great pleasure from it, they became more centered, more confident, and generally happier. Whether it would lead to other things is moot; the magic had already taken place.

What would it take to have this depth of sexual experience? You can be sure that some of the people watching that exchange would have thought of her as a harlot or a slut, "And she, a nurse!" Tsk, tsk, tsk! The "panel of judges" would be having a field day. Of course, the panel of judges had probably never had a sexual experience the likes of which they just watched, so it stands to reason that they would try to limit it!

What would it take for you to be in allowance of sex? Of being sexual? How willing would you be to receive all that can be created through sex with no judgments or points of view?

Asking these questions in a roomful of people generates a whole variety of responses based on old judgments and points of view around the wrongness of what had occurred. Where do you think you would be in that conversation? If you had any hint of "Why, I never…!", you might want to do a little "interesting point of view" housekeeping.

Unfortunately, within the multitude of rigid points of view and judgments, sex is referred to as dirty, base, animal behavior, sinful, immoral and otherwise disgusting from all directions. There are an endless number of taboos about sex, such as the taboo against allowing anyone to know that you have sex organs, and you must certainly not let anyone see them! Why, you are not allowed to even name them, so you've got to come up with some acceptable synonyms for vagina or penis. Cock, tally-whacker, pee-pee, dick, and on and on and on. You're fine in most circles if you simply don't use the word penis. Female parts are just as silly: beaver, muff, box, boobs, knockers, and on and on and on. Everyone knows tons of euphemisms for various parts of the body that are in the "unmentionables" category. Nipples. Would everyone in the room who doesn't have nipples please raise your hands? And yet we have difficulty talking about nipples because we have been infused with the wrongness of talking about sex.

So, we find the judgment that our bodies are nasty, unclean, bad, corrupt and shameful. Shame on you for having body parts! No wonder movies with naked bodies in them are referred to as dirty movies. And, feeling as though we carry "scarlet letters" on our chests, we try to deal with our own sexualness. To the extent that we buy the judgments about sexuality, our lives and relationships will be limited and stilted by them. Do you suppose that "performance anxiety" is tied to a judgment? Who has the authority to judge your sexual performance? If you answered, no one, including yourself, you win the prize. Sex isn't a contest. It's a creative expression of a person's being. Ever feel guilty about

118

sex? Too much, not enough, not good enough to please a partner? Guilt is an offshoot of shame, and shame around sex is deeply rooted in most people. Judgment and shame usually fit together like a horse and carriage and guilt is the padlock on the corral that was built around your life to limit you.

A rite of passage throughout childhood seems to be a child receiving misinformation and disinformation – outright lies about bodies and sex. Hair on the palms and having to wear glasses as the result of masturbating comes to mind. It's almost as if parents are afraid of telling their children, openly, honestly and without judgment, what is happening to them as they grow. There is also the fact that children must honor and obey adults. Period. What they're told by an adult must be true.

A little boy of about five years old was over at his neighbor's house, playing with a little girl there. At one point, their play brought them into the little girl's closet, where they spontaneously started to play "you show me yours, and I'll show you mine." The little boy had just dropped his drawers and the little girl was starting to explore more closely when the door flew open and the little girl's mother pulled them into the room, shrieking, "What are you doing? Shame on you!" The little boy had an " out-of-body experience;" he couldn't even talk. He froze. The little girl was in the corner wide-eyed and whimpering. The girl's mother looked at the boy, who was just buttoning up his pants and ordered him to go home and tell his mother exactly what *he* had done!

It wasn't that far, but the little boy took very small steps as he headed home. He tiptoed into the dining room where his mother sat at the table and, when she saw him, she asked, "What happened? Are you all right?" He told her every detail of his encounter because he was scared to death that the girl's mother would grill his mother and find out he hadn't, and he didn't want to think about the consequences. When he finished telling her, she gently pulled him to her and gave him a hug and said: "It's okay. Little boys and girls sometimes do that." She then went on to explain to him why it's not a good idea to do more of that, at least until he's older.

What messages were received here? Sex is awful and if you do anything sexual, you will be punished for it. You can be forgiven for the sin of sex if you forgo it until some later date. Date and time to be announced. The sin that was committed here was that the two children would learn about how one another's bodies worked. That was only one episode in the development of the children's sense of sexual self. If it's sex, you have to hide it.

Children start developing their images of sex and sexualness long before their bodies have matured enough to be actively sexual. Physical maturity normally begins at around 12 years old, a few years either way for most children. It takes time for them to fully develop sexually. How many parents start gearing up to have "the talk" with their kids only as they approach sexual maturity indicated by body hair and smelly armpits? Little do they know that the child has already crossed that bridge.

The kids know why the bedroom door is locked and whisper about it to each other, usually inaccurately. They know that there is fun or tension and arguing around sex, or something else that they sense, but don't see. Children know that their sex organs are "private" and must not be touched unnecessarily lest the child become aroused, something that happens from a very early age as every mother who has changed her little boy's diapers knows. In the process of cleaning him up, she stimulates the little penis, which causes a tiny erection, right before he pees on her. Seems kind of unfair. Touching feels really, really good! But it isn't allowed! Mom pulls his hand away as he tries to do it himself.

The problem with all of this is that the information that the kids receive is what they see and hear and deduce. If you put yourself in that position, you'd find that it's all very confusing. That's good. That's bad. That's really bad! Their little minds start sorting out the badness of being sexual, but never seem to learn about the joy of being sexual except in the dark, in a closet, under covers. Even then, as the little boy and girl in the story demonstrated, someone will find them, even in the closet.

Perhaps the most destructive part of this is that little kids playing "doctor" are controlled by the use of shame. "You're not doing anything nasty, are you?" Shame, shame, shame. Shame is an ugly tool for controlling people. Once a person has been shamed, it seems to stay with them forever unless they themselves remove it. If the same shaming is done persistently, it works itself more and more deeply into the child's (or anyone's) sense of being. They become "damaged goods" in their own minds. Most of the judgments concerning sex center around shame, and that carries over into relationships, and this is where disaster erupts.

Is it possible that some of this shame made it into your ideas of sex and sexualness? Do you reflexively hide your body so nobody can see it? This would be a good time to go into question and ask, "How have I and others shamed me to the point that my being and my sexualness is limited, taking away my joy, self-love and self-esteem?" Go into allowance of those things that pop up and the judgments that go with them. It's all simply an "interesting point of view," and it's an interesting point of view that I bought those points of view. Keep doing it over a period of time; you'll know when it's time to quit. You won't feel the drain from the energy of those shameful judgments.

While most of the intense judgments are directed at sexual activities, the messages concerning gender are woven throughout the defining sex in its narrow, limiting form. What do you suppose the two kids who were found in the closet learned about sexual identity? Did the little boy get the message that it was all his fault because males are stronger and impose themselves on females? If that were not the case, why was he the one that took all the scolding? Did the girl come to see herself as the "weaker sex" needing to be protected from aggressive males? What if she were the one who grabbed the little boy's hand and pulled him into the closet (just as likely as the other way around). What lifelong gender identities are created in this sort of scenario?

It's interesting that for many adults, the thought of the little girl being interested in sex is not as likely to show up as that of the little boy. Already, a tacit point of view develops about the gender roles of girls and boys. "All you boys think about is sex!" Is this true? Is this a judgable offense? Does this mean that girls don't think about sex? What judgments do girls who think about sex receive? Reminiscent of ballroom dancing, where the man leads and the woman follows, do the same rules apply to sex?

Very many cultures have a mixed view of sex. In some places, it is simply something that is normal for people to do and everybody, including children, understands the whole business. There is no mystery; it's just part of living. In other places, sex is treated as a lust-inspired and uncontrollable urge, and it is shameful unless done by the rules set down by this or that elder, based on a huge number of just plain crazy judgments and points of view about sex.

Remember "bundling boards"? During the 18th century, in British North American colonies, bundling was a practice in which an unmarried couple would share a bed for the night. Fully clothed and having promised not to engage in sex during the night. To enforce this rule, a board was attached to the bedstead, head and foot, running down the middle to separate the couple being bundled. If they failed to carry through as requested, and the woman became pregnant, the couple was required to marry. There were other unusual devices utilized to control sex at the time, such as the chastity belt and the courting tube, a long tube through which the courting couple could converse without being heard by others. Controlling a young woman's sexual behaviors was a part of enforcing the "thou shalt have no sex before marriage" law. The point here is that sex has never been about one man and one woman without interference, whether from institutions or relatives.

Bear in mind that sexual urges are hard-wired into our brains and, unless something drastic happens, we will respond in some manner to stimuli: our loins tingle, the pitch of our voice goes up, we talk fast, we take shallow breaths; things like that. Stimuli are brought to the brain via our senses, any of which can stimulate a sexual response. A smell or sound can be just as stimulating as touch or sight. We each have our own receptors that arrange themselves in an infinite set of configurations.

Some people have been so programmed by powerful social points of view and judgments that they suppress their sexual urges completely. More than just the sexual urges are purged, with that purging a significant part of a person's personality and energy seem to disappear. Some people seem to be able to function like this, many do not.

It's kind of like air pollution. You might not even smell it, but you breathe it in nonetheless. That would be a good question to use for approaching allowance of your sexualness, "How many points of view have I been taking in unaware like breathing, which cause me to judge myself and others about sex?" Interesting point of view that I have those points of view. Interesting point of view that I was unaware of those points of view and bought them without thought.

You may just be amazed at how stilted your attitude about sex is because you were carrying those judgments. Even if your sex life is satisfactory by your estimation, what if it could be mind-blowingly better? Sometimes sex doesn't work as planned. Can you experience that without lapsing into judgment? He thought go right; she thought go left, and they got off the track and disappointment showed up and people were unhappy. Could you handle that without judgment? (The definition of allowance is to be willing to experience everything, the good, the bad and the "that's a real bummer!") There will be other chances to experience bliss, especially if this experience was managed without points of view and judgment.

Some questions to explore: What is wrong with loving my body and loving myself and sharing with a partner? How did the sin of sex take root in me? What would happen if I rid myself of all judgments about sex? What does creative sex look like and what would happen if I did that? There are a lot more questions waiting to be asked. Interesting point of view that I suppressed my freedom to ask questions about sex.

CHAPTER 15:

Allowance and Sex
Part II

S it down alone for a while and ask some questions about how many of the points of view and judgments you carry about you and sex are yours. Often, specific scenes from your past will show up and you will feel the effect of the judgments in your belly. How many people shamed you for something to do with your learning about sex, either as a child or an adult. Interesting point of view that they drove home to you the vileness of your thoughts and acts, and interesting point of view that you bought them as yours. Interesting point of view that you borrowed the judgments that other people had for themselves and made them yours.

If all of those burning fixed points of view about your body and sex were extinguished by allowance, you could do sex by choice. You could be comfortable with your feelings and desires without having to judge yourself or your partner. To find out how few or how many judgments you have, examine those things that "push your buttons" when sex comes up in a conversation. Do you consider the subject good or bad? Do you align and agree with the conversation or do you react to it negatively? Does discussing sex bring to mind unhappy, negative, or ugly scenes that you try not to remember? Interesting point of view that I carry all of that, allowing it to limit all the joyous freedom of my sexuality I could have. Interesting point of view that I am obligated to carry all the pain and regret of the things I won't allow myself to be rid of. Am I really obligated to carry those memories and their pain? Are all the judgments contained in that real?

Remember that sexualness itself is not a rational process; it is driven by the body much more than by the mind. Your body responds to the energy of those around you. If you come within range of someone whose sexual energy is being broadcast, your body will pick it up. Should that person's eyes meet yours in admiration, your body will be aware and react. Your heartbeat quickens, you feel a tingle in your groin, you start leaning toward the source of the energy, all without thought. Your voice will change, as will your choice of words. Not everybody's sexual energy will be attractive to you and when that happens, your body won't respond, and you'll move on.

The energy of admiration and attraction has a profound effect on the body and your body will respond. In actuality, it could be your body that likes to be admired and is encouraging a reaction. Everywhere that you are not in allowance of being with someone who admires you that much, you eliminate the possibility of experiencing that in your life. The point here is not whether you sleep with someone out of the ordinary, but whether or not you are in judgment of what might happen there. If you have no point of view here, you have choice.

Allowance is the place where you're willing to receive everything in life and therefore create more living than you have now. I am certainly not saying that you *have* to have sex with whomever desires you. You can always choose what will work for you. I am simply asking you to look at what is actually going on in each moment of your life and what your actions create. Try to step out of the immediate judgments of the right and wrong of sex and see where you are functioning from. When your life is limited by the judgments of *who* you will not receive, that becomes *what* you will not receive. If your body would like to be admired, let yourself know that! If you want to create more living, you've got to be in allowance.

You could ask your body, "Body, do you want to have sex with this person?" If the answer is yes, you could say to the person, "Hey. Do you want to go home and have sex?" Of course, most people don't do that. Why? Because it's "just not done by decent people!" It's not appropriate. And it does nothing to create a relationship. And other points of view. Maybe so, but the body is happy. You've got to look at things from a slightly different direction and be in allowance of what makes your life easy.

A woman once asked me, "What about men wanting me for sex only and not caring?" Well, interesting point of view that they want you for sex. Do you *have* to have sex with someone just because they want you? No. But this woman almost always did. She liked being wanted. If somebody created the energy of wanting her, then she figured she must be in the right place. And, at the same time, she had the point of view that, because there were so many, she couldn't say yes to everyone. When I pointed out that she could say no to everyone, out came a major point of view that she had been functioning from: "It's all going to turn out great in the future."

She was choosing to go with men who would screw her over to maintain the point of view that "someday my prince will come." She was not asking for what would actually work for her; instead, she held onto a romantic ideal. Rather than looking for her "prince," what if she were to simply ask, "Who would be the most fun person for me to have as a bed mate?"

A man went on a date with a woman he had met, and the next day caught himself thinking, "I wonder what our house will be like and how many children we will have." Then he thought, "Wait a minute! What am I doing? I don't even know this woman's last name. I haven't kissed her. I haven't had sex with her. And I'm creating a whole life with her? I'm nuts!" And he realized he needed to do things a little differently. Was he there to have sex or to cement his future dream life with this almost complete stranger?

What if you could simply enjoy sex? Ask yourself who would be *fun* to have sex with…not who will be your love that you'll go happily ever after into the sunset and live together with forever. So many people don't actually want a relationship, with all that entails, but they do want romance. I understand the desire for romance, but the lure of romance can keep us from creating what works.

We sometimes use romance to avoid the ability to create the kind of relationship that will actually work for us. This is just insane! We could choose a more pragmatic approach to creating what we would actually enjoy. For example, if romance is what you desire, you could say, "Okay, I *love*

131

romance, but I do not desire this, or this, or this. How can I get what I truly desire?"

The majority of people are not in allowance of sex or relationships. They don't use the tool "interesting point of view" for all their points of view about sex and relationships. This means that they don't actually have to be present in the creation of their own lives.

Have you ever truly looked at what you truly desire? Would you like somebody who's good to have sex with? Or somebody who will be there for you? Do you want somebody to go to romantic movies with you and hold your hand? Do you want somebody you can take on picnics and family outings and have everyone love them?

You could ask how many people you would need to have in your life in order to have all of these things. You see, most people in search of a relationship keep trying to make one person fulfill *all* roles. But no one person can fulfill *all* roles. Instead, you might ask for multiple people to show up in your life to fulfill all the roles you desire; whatever actually works for you! That's allowance.

You've got to have allowance of whatever your point of view is, even if it's not like anybody else's, rather than make it wrong and hide from yourself what it is that you actually desire to create. So many people try to make it wrong to be who they are.

Instead, they could realize how who they are is what's going to create everything.

What else is actually possible?

There is no emotional reaction to being asked to have sex with someone in allowance; sex and all the things that go with it are simply part of living on the planet. If a judgment or point of view shows up, the person uses interesting point of view, almost without thinking, and bats it out of his or her life. These people have an ever-changing view of what they desire sex to be for them. It's everchanging because they're ever-changing. They don't really need to go looking for variety or freshness in their sex lives, because their lives are filled with variety and freshness instead of combatting judgments.

To someone who is filled with points of view about sex that they've bought hook, line, and sinker, just bringing it up as a serious topic will bring out of them a reaction of some kind. There is neither time nor paper enough to write all of the reactions, but some examples might be in order. To begin, you might ask where the judgments and points of view came from.

Sex sells. It sells everything from cars to liquor to house paint. Why? Why is it possible to influence someone to buy something by simply alluding to sex? Or perhaps a better way of describing it, what buttons does the consumer get pushed by teasing with glimpses of a sexy body, or a couple walking

133

off camera suggesting that they were headed off to have sex?

Earlier on, anger was brought up; anger and the "buttons" that can trigger an angry outburst. If a person is watching television and something that comes across the screen triggers a button, the viewer will suddenly become angry. You'll notice that it is not a rational response; suddenly the anger is there with no explanation. What we call anger is associated with some major hormonal discharges that take place given appropriate stimulus, and the body reacts. Nothing is really rational here. Anger hits! And then the rubble needs to be cleared away.

Sexual arousal hits in just the same way as anger. Given the proper stimulus, – visual, tactile, olfactory, or auditory – the buttons are there waiting to be engaged. Again, it is not a rational process. Hormones are discharged, the brain shuts off and the body looks for action. If anger is a powerful part of what we are, so is sex. Although, sex is more pleasant, the urge can be just as strong as anger.

What would it take to uncomplicate sex? What would it take to associate sex with fun, sharing, gifting and receiving? What points of view have you bought that say that it's all about giving, never about receiving? What would sex be like without points of view and judgments about us, our bodies and our sex?

134

Chapter 16:

Allowance and Physical Pain

O ur bodies have sense organs that guide us around the planet, a job for which they are well suited. They have extremely sensitive guidance systems that are always running; our ears, nose, tastebuds, skin, and eyes pick up information and send it along to the brain, the pilot, for processing.

Another function of our bodies is to act like a receiver, picking up energy that is broadcast by others. If you enter a room where someone is truly angry, whether acting it out or not, you are liable to feel yourself tense up, and want to leave without a real explanation as to why. Anger is energy that is broadcast in all directions. Most often, people deny that they have been affected by that anger and go about their business while pretending to be untouched, all the while having a tightening of the solar plexus that is indicative of fear or their own anger.

Less apparent, people also have a sense of what is going on in someone else's body. In fact, it's not farfetched that they might be *more* aware of others' pains than they are of their own. That lack of awareness about their own body creates a situation where pains that they empathically (but not often consciously) pick up are pains from others and, because they can "feel" it with their bodies, they immediately come to the conclusion that it is theirs.

What if the pain isn't theirs? What if they are simply accepting the projected pain into their body and, feeling it, come to the conclusion that it is theirs, much the way they'd buy a point of view or a judgment? It is the conclusions and points of view we come to about the pain we feel that create the difficulties.

Nearly everyone can make a connection between an attitude or point of view and bodily pain. Tension-producing points of view like "I have to…" or "I'll die if I don't…" are triggers that invoke people's fight or flight emotions; however, there isn't any place for those emotions to be fully expressed physically, so they start the body to produce pain. While this is metaphorical, our first thoughts about a cause for stomach ulcers is an overload of stress. Another place that this shows up is in the back which is a repository for tension that presents itself as pain.

We have two different sets of pain each of which need to be addressed if we would like to be rid of them, our pain and that of others. Our pain is usually tied to a point of view that holds it in place within us. You might have observed a child holding an "owie" on his finger and limping to find some parental sympathy. Mom kisses the owie and puts a little bandage on it and, miraculously, the child's limp disappears! It might just be possible that the limp was garnish for the hurt finger being used to squeeze sympathy and hugging from her. If you look around, you will undoubtedly see adults doing similar things.

What if this little child clung to the limp and made it important? Why? Because it invariably yields results: "Poor baby." You could ask yourself, "How useful is the pain I have created?" When we create those pains, they actually do hurt. Some people with longstanding pains are sometimes diagnosed as hypochondriacs. A hypochondriac actually does hurt. The pain is considered hypochondriacal because no physical cause can be found.

In order to keep ourselves tied up in our pains, we simply need to be unaware of what's really going on. On the other hand, to rid ourselves of self-induced pain, we need to ask some questions: Is this pain real? (If you stab your knee with an ice pick, the pain is real!)

To begin getting rid of unwanted pain from others, we might ask a question such as "Does this pain belong to me?" If it doesn't, it is a point of view. An "interesting point of view" at that! In response to class participant who was wondering about allowance and physical pain, I asked her if she was in allowance of her pain. She reported that, though she would like to say yes, a lot of the time she was not. I then asked if her pain was hers in the first place, or if she was trying to make it her pain when it wasn't. She immediately recognized that the pain was not hers and that she was indeed making it hers.

Now, why would someone do that? For her, turning the awareness she was having with her body into her pain was limiting what she could do. But, in a way, that was actually working for her. It was proving the point of view that she had been given by her mother that everybody has to suffer. In her case, chronic pain was at least partially the result of her mother's point of view. She was proving that her mother's point of view was right, and that her mother was right, so that she could feel deserving of the money she was going to get from her mother. Amazing!

People spend a great deal of time trying to rid their bodies of pain. The degree to which pain and illness appear in people's lives is apparent in television commercials where anyone with "moderate to severe" something needs to buy and take a remedy, which brings with it a "Pandora's box" filled with side effects that can be worse than the original malady. They present everything, from chronic back pain to gastric problems, to heaven knows what else.

Many of them describe themselves as having healing gifts. When they meet with their subjects, there will be pain, physical, emotional and mental, projected during the healing session, and the healer uses whatever arts and skills they know to remove the pain and its causes. The problem is that during the process, many of these people remove the infirmity in the person they're working with, only to have it appear in their own bodies. It gives some credence to the tales of the wounded healers.

There is much talk today about empathy and the lack thereof. The world would be a better place, people say, if we could feel one another's pains; walk a mile in their shoes. This might just be true, but the word empathy might not be the best choice for the process. It might be more accurate to use awareness to describe the ability to sense what other people have going on. The old tales about empaths talk about the healer actually removing the offending cause of the pain and taking it into themselves—walking a mile in another's shoes. The problem there is that if empaths take too much of the pain and take it on themselves, it might well cause them to die; or so the tale goes.

When we ask our bodies, "Does this pain belong to me?" It just might not. Try it. If you live in a city of a million people, how much of other people's pain would you take in? Especially during troubled times, where pain floats through the streets like the angel of death. If you find yourself feeling sad, angry, afraid, or suddenly have pain in your body, ask! Is this mine? If it belongs to someone else, you can say "return to sender." People sometimes hesitate to do this, not wanting to harm anyone, but what you receive and send back is not pain. Rather it is the idea and energy of pain. You won't hurt the sender; and you will help yourself a lot! Be in allowance of your pain. It's simply an interesting point of view. Remembering that will bring you to awareness of how to deal with the pain. Your unheeding sensitivity might just be bringing you the tragedies of others which is mutually destructive.

We use all of these points of view to create what is showing up in our lives. This is why you might want to use the tool "interesting point of view" with *everything*. This particular woman had been using it with the pains, but not with *everything*. By focusing on the pains, she was looking to shift the effect of her points of view rather than shifting the underlying points of view themselves. She could ask questions such as, "What about me am I using

140

to attract other people's pains?" and " How am I creating a reality that is filled with pain?" It's all interesting point of view.

Another class participant reached out complaining of body pains. She stated that she takes a lot of crap from her environment and has to protect herself so that she has everything in harmony. She presented this and asked what she could do to change it.

Where was the question in any of that? She had already decided that the conflict was real. She had already decided that she had pain. There was no question there. She was not in allowance; she was not in question. If you're not in question, you can't have allowance. You've got to look at, "What part is true? What part is real? What part am I making real that isn't?"

A common reaction to a toxic environment is to feel vulnerable, which leads to the desire to protect or defend yourself. When you feel that way, what kind of barriers do you put up? What kinds of walls do you hide behind that don't change anything, but damage you rather than the source of the toxicity? Walls are a solidification of energy. In other words, they are judgments in solid form. While the desire was for protection, the walls end up trapping you. If you go into allowance in the situation, where it's all an interesting point of view, two things are liable to happen. First, the "toxic energy" is liable to flow around you, without harming you and, secondly, you will be able to choose a course of action based on the possibilities you create at the time.

Recognize that nothing is real unless you make it so. Nothing is right. Nothing is good. Nothing is anything but what you decide it is. You're the most powerful being on the planet. You *can* create more than you may ever choose to admit. Yet so many people go, "I can't do this!"

We create everything that shows up for us with the points of view we take. And then we buy it all and make it real and true when it isn't the only possibility. Stop that! Let yourself be interesting point of view about everything you've decided is true. "Interesting point of view that I think this is true." Why would you think anything was true? Oh, because you *decided* it was, and once you decide something it's set in concrete forever. Or is it? Really, it's up to you what you would like to choose.

Some people find the notion that we choose our own misfortunes, like pain, hard-heartedness or cynicism. That's an interesting point of view associated with our addiction to taking care of others at all costs to ourselves. One way to think about this is, would you be a better functioning citizen of the world if you were free from the solidified energies of judgments about yourself, others and the world? Probably. Would you like your ambulance attendant to show up with an arm in a cast and using crutches? Probably not. Everyone benefits when you are in allowance.

142

CHAPTER 17:

Allowance and Other People

In the 21st century, the people of the world have become more and more contentious. It's almost as if there is a "contention vendor" somewhere, who sells a variety of points of view to choose from that would be a basis for polarization. Religious, political, gender, racial, or moral polarity, and a host of others would be the vendor's wares. To "buy" such points of view changes a person. "Them or us" mentality becomes the norm, as if we always have to have an adversary or an enemy. The subject of the contention is not really significant; what is significant is the points of view that become hardened like concrete. People, friends and neighbors, scream at one another everywhere and even come to blows over their differences. Within a single family there is likely to be a "line in the sand" drawn and household members either shout at one another or remain unspeaking in separate parts of the house. If, as you read this, you become uncomfortable, you more than likely have bought a point of view that you now feel is threatened.

The root of this situation is not that people have varying views of the world; that has always been the case. For whatever reason, people have found it necessary to make their views unchangeable reflections of themselves and a conversation about those views would suddenly become a personal attack on them, which they are compelled to defend. Instead of defending your views or attacking another's, recognizing that it's all an interesting point of view removes you from the intensity of it all, yet allows others to live as they choose.

Take a look at the ways you align and agree and resist and react to others. Suppose people around you are incessantly spouting opposing viewpoints and will challenge you to your face, daring you to react or disagree. Whether you align and agree, or resist and react to their confrontation, it is not a very comfortable exchange. What would happen if you went into allowance, where you could hear, or even talk about someone's fixed beliefs and judgments without taking on any of the energy of their fixed points of view? It is actually easier to do allowance with someone who has a point of view that you

144

wouldn't align and agree with. It is simple to say to a viewpoint counter to yours that it is an interesting point of view. However, if you share all or part of such a viewpoint, the tendency will be to align or agree with it, which leads to places you'd rather not go as those agreements, judgments bought and swallowed, would likely have a profound effect on you, just as limiting as the other option. What would your life be like if you were to allow yourself to be aware of everything – the good, the bad, and the ugly – without a point of view?

In allowance, you would be aware of yourself and any reactions as well as the actual messages being spewed in your direction in a discussion like those above. That awareness allows you to use interesting point of view to make sure that you aren't buying something you don't wish to buy. In times of divisiveness, such as the present, people who are polar opposites tend to gather like iron filings at the end of a magnet. There is always a space between the groups. There is usually a giant tug-of-war going on, trying to get people to move from one pole to the other. If you happen to agree with one side, would you find yourself proselytizing in an attempt to make sure that other people agree with the wonderful tenets of your movement? People often see changing others' points of view as their personal job or holy grail. If you find yourself doing that, it might be time to stand back and check out your allowance. We really don't have a mandate to change other people's thinking or judgments. It doesn't help them; it hurts us.

Allowance is the willingness to receive any and all energies without the judgments that obscure your awareness. When you have allowance of other people, you can simply see what they are choosing without having to be at the effect of their doing so. You are not limited to the choices others make. And, beyond that, if you are in allowance of the choices others are making, you can be aware of what's going on in each situation and choose what you would like to choose to create the life and world you would like to create. With total allowance you can have total awareness. And when you have total awareness, you have the freedom to create anything, even more than you may have ever imagined possible.

A participant in a class once asked what to do when she is with someone who is really making themselves wrong. She was wondering how not to align and agree with the point of view that that person was wrong so as not to beat them up. She said that she was using the tool of interesting point of view, but that she still felt pulled into this dynamic. Ultimately, it seemed that she was not really doing interesting point of view at all. Instead, she was trying to figure out what she could align and agree with or resist and react to, rather than going, "Interesting point of view, that's their point of view. Why would I even think that point of view had any value?"

Her point of view was that the person in question was being mean to themselves and that she wanted to save them or get them to change. This point of view was based on the assumption that if she could save them then they would be better off. That is not having allowance for them *not* to choose something besides being mean to themselves. It is believing that if they *could* choose something else then they *would* choose something else.

Rather than asking if the person *can* choose something else, ask if they *will*. These are two totally different questions. Don't assume that someone *will* just because they *can*. For example, a man who always has the point of view, "That person could have such a bigger and better life!" When he was asked, "What makes you think they are going to choose it?" He responded, "Well, I knew I could have a better life, so I continuously chose to create a better life." The big question here is, "And have they chosen to have a bigger and better life?" No, they haven't, but my friend doesn't understand why they wouldn't choose that if they could. The answer is simple: because they don't! That's it. No big reason or justification. It is simply a choice.

We always have the choice to choose greater. The question is, *will* we choose something greater? What would it be like if *you* actually did? Most people don't. Allowance here is realizing that a person *can* choose something else, but will they? If not, that's okay. Never mind. Make your next choice with the awareness of what they will choose. If you keep looking for a little window of possibility for them to choose something else, just be aware of the idiocy in that. Be in allowance of your idiocy wherever it may show up. Recognize what points of view you are using to make your choices and let yourself be aware of all that is actually occurring. Ask yourself, "Will this person actually choose this?" If they won't, what would you like to choose next?

Allowance is a muscle you're developing. You may find that at times it is easier to use that muscle than at other times. It's okay. Keep working on it until it becomes your fallback position for living and awareness. Ask yourself, "What energy, space, consciousness, and choice can I be to have total clarity and ease and absolute allowance with this for all eternity?" Not being able to instantly go to allowance is not a wrongness. This is a skill that must be practiced. Choose and practice being in allowance of everything that shows up, both with yourself and with others.

Chapter 18:

Allowance and Your Family

D id your family seek to define, confine, and control you instead of encouraging you to create everything in your life greater than they had? "You can't be an artist, for Pete's sake, they don't make any money! You need to help this family run the business, just like I did with my dad!" Often the process of limiting will be under the radar, and you won't be aware that it is happening. Did your family define itself in terms like, "We're poor, but we're honest."? "We're all good at English, but none of us can do math. We can't ever reconcile our check book!"

Most parents will try their hardest to raise their kids in the "right" way and be "good" parents. There is no handbook for being a parent, so usually the only guidance they have is what they learned from their own parents. To make matters cloudier, there is no such thing as good or bad parents. Good and bad are judgments, so if you eliminate them, you are left with just parents.

The rights and wrongs of being a parent differs widely. There was a man who loved his wife and family dearly. He grew up roping livestock on a ranch full of fairly hard men. They had to be hard because conditions were hard. Knowing that his son would have to be tough in order to survive, as he'd had to, his relationship with his son was one of strictness and rigidity.

One day the son, about 14 years old, was riding his motorcycle in front of the house when he took a tumble over the handlebars and, with a loud yelp fell flat on his back. As he lay there, sobbing in pain and shock, his dad came out and yelled: "Stop your damn bawling!" The boy just sobbed louder, so his dad took off his belt and began to whip him with it, telling him that when he stopped crying the beating would stop. The crying did stop. In fact, according to his proud father, the boy never did that "baby-crying" again.

Good dad or bad dad? In the dad's mind was the overriding belief that he had to raise his child to be tough if the boy were to survive. His point of view was honest, and he lived according to what he thought to be true. What points of view does this story bring up for you? What emotions and energy attached to that point of view have you bought? How are those points of view limiting your life? If you go into allowance about this incident, are you afraid that you are condoning the dad's behavior? The child's? Interesting point of view that you have that point of view. From a place of allowance, you are free to act as you choose. Turn the dad over to a child protection agency? Ignore the incident? Have a serious talk with the dad? You are free to act as you choose. Your actions are not of real significance to you when you are asked the question; your judgments are. In allowance, free of the judgments and fixed points of view, you are free to act from a place of rationality, not from the points of view you bought in the past.

If your parents were dysfunctional, where did that come from? Their parents? If that is the case, from where did grandma and grandpa's dysfunctions arise? It goes back farther and farther into the past. In what way could you contribute to the cessation of that dysfunctional legacy? Did all those people in the past carry with them a bagful of judgments and points of view, as did the cowboy above, that guided their lives?

Detaching from the litany of judgments that were handed down from parent to child is necessary to become aware of what is actually happening in the present and go into allowance. You do not need to work yourself into an early grave because your grandfather was a hard worker. You are free to choose the work life you desire because the determining factor will not be the family's belief in grandpa's point of view. Think about the points of view your family was functioning from. Have you been aligning and agreeing with or resisting and reacting to any of those points of view?

Allowance can be a pragmatic way to be aware of the workings of your family and to open the door for possibilities you may never have considered. But remember, when you give yourself the gift of allowance, this does not mean you have to simply accept everyone's insanity. It is, rather, what allows you to know where people are functioning from and to use that awareness to create something else.

One of the reasons that people have trouble getting out from under the "family name" is that there are two sets of judgments. Do you have judgments of your family? Do they have judgments of you? It might seem easier to look at the family judgments of you and deal with them, than to find your judgments of them and deal with them. Both sets of judgments affect you to the same degree.

As we've explored, allowance is being able to see what is and have no point of view about it. This includes every thought, feeling, emotion, opinion, judgment, conclusion, and more that is a part of each and every situation. When you allow yourself to be aware of all aspects of a situation – even the judgments involved – the choices available to you open up. If, however, you do not acknowledge what is actually going on, you will continue to be directed by the points of view, and leave yourself ignorant of what you and those whose points of view you bought are trying to accomplish. Because judgments tend to be energetically heavy, you won't be able to create your life with the ease that is possible for you.

Often, people attempt to use judgments as a way to control one another. A class participant once related that she had difficulty being in allowance of her daughter and that she was quick to be judgmental. Basically, this woman was trying to control her daughter to get her to turn out the way she (the mother) wanted her to, rather than letting the daughter do with her life what she chose. The mother was not asking questions about the life her daughter wanted to create.

Another mother spoke up about the fact that her son was playing a lot of video games and how it was not working for her. In describing the situation, she brought out a bunch of conclusions, all of which made her right and her son wrong. "He's never going to amount to anything if all he does is play those games on the computer!" "I want him to be happy instead of being a zombie, chained to a computer!" "When I want him to clean his room, or haul out the trash, he says 'Okay, Mom', and goes on playing the game. He's more attached to that stupid video game than he is to his family!" "I can't get him to stop! I think he's addicted!"

In both examples, the mothers were operating from judgments and points of view that many parents share. If I don't make my child act according to the rules set out by parents everywhere, I will be a bad mother. Children are supposed to listen to and respect their parents and to do what they're told. Because the children, in these instances, didn't do this, both mothers bought the idea that they were somehow wrong. They saw themselves as weak, ineffective, and unable to make their children behave as they "should." If these two mothers sat down and just thought about the judgments they were buying and creating both about themselves and their children, some clarity might emerge. "Am I really a bad mom if…?" "Is my child going to be worthless as an adult because…?" If they applied interesting points of view to such questions, there would be significant changes in their lives.

When they became aware of what they were doing, allowance for the judgments and conclusions that *they* were functioning from began to get them out of the right and wrong of their points of view and into the creation of different possibilities. Both mothers became more open to negotiating something that would work for both their child and themselves.

154

This may all sound overly simple, especially with a topic as heavy and significant as family. But what if it actually could be that simple? Is there anything that you have not been acknowledging about your family, that if you acknowledged it, would set you free to create what actually works for you?

If you're going to create beyond the limitations of your family, your friends, your culture, your country, and all the other points of view you have developed that limit you, you will have to choose to be aware. Remember that allowance is a choice that creates a way to outstrip anyone or anything that wants to confine you, define you, or contain you. You need never be contained by anybody. Never be stopped. You are in allowance; you are always free to create greater possibilities in your life!

Most people are a bit coy about admitting they created something, fearing that they and their creation will be judged inadequate. In this case, though, it is important to recognize that when you create something – and this happens in all areas of our lives – you must be in allowance of the fact that you created it. Again, acknowledge the fact that you created it! And then, if you wish, you can choose to change what you created. If you deny to yourself that you created something, how could you go about changing it? Not every choice is going to be what you really wanted, but if you own those that aren't, you can change your mind and choose something else. No penalty. No judgment.

Our families have the possibility to be our greatest sources of love and support, or they can be the source of the chains that drag us down. If you become aware of what your upbringing with your family truly was, as well as what your current relationship with them is, you can choose something of your own design.

CHAPTER 19:

Allowance for Other People's Choices

You may have noticed that when you chose to do or be or create something and shared it with friends and family, you received a chorus of conflicting points of view about your choice. "My brother tried to invest in that, and he lost all his money. I don't think that I'd invest there." His brother is a plumber, not necessarily a financial planner. "My sister married a guy from New York and the marriage didn't last a year!" Of course, where a person is from doesn't have anything to do with their suitability as a marriage partner. That's absurd. No matter what your choices are, you will be set upon by a host of people who feel qualified to run your life.

Are you among the closet experts who feel qualified to guide people through making choices? Before giving someone advice, you'd have to make a judgment of the choice—good, bad, right, wrong. Once you've got your judgment in place, you can begin stating your position and why your point of view would be best for the person who brought it up. In fact, you might feel obligated to weigh in on the rightness or wrongness of the person's choice.

Now, trade places with the person sharing their choice. What is it like to share something important to you and find that, rather than being engaged in a mutual sharing, you are treated as though you are standing before a panel of judges? Some of the judges are uplifting and positive, but judges, nonetheless. Some of them will be sour and negative about your choices and tell you why at great length.

In either position, there is judgment being thrown about that is potentially problematic for you in either role. To keep from being eviscerated by the knives of judgment, the first step is to start being aware of what's happening. Ask yourself, "What's really happening here?" "Why is this making me uncomfortable?," questions that will clarify things. Once you begin to really see what's happening, it's time to engage "interesting point of view." It's an interesting point of view that they think I'm unqualified for what I chose, and it's an interesting point of view that I bought their judgments.

When someone describes a choice they made or something that's happening in their lives, do you see it as it really is, or do you take the overall concept and apply your own points of view to it? When you try to tell someone about your gallstone removal, even those who have never had a gallstone removed will have something to say about the experience. None of those people know what *your* experience was.

There seems a compulsion for people to describe an appendectomy in all its gory detail, hopping from listener to listener. "Did you hear about my appendectomy?" What is gained by doing that? What does the person doing the describing hope to gain from the listeners? Or perhaps, what is the "hollow spot" that the person has that needs to be filled with the opinions, points of view or judgment of others? If there were not a need there, what would compel the person to talk about it?

The truth is, nobody can fill the hollow spot but you. It isn't filled and healed by taking notes on other people's sympathy (judgment) or advice (point of view). It is healed by going into the question and using allowance. "What is this empty place in me that I am trying to fill by having other people feel sorry for me or advise me?" "Is the empty place real?" Interesting point of view that, even though it never works, I keep running to others to fix my empty feeling. Interesting point of view that I have that feeling. Interesting point of view that I value the judgments and points of view of others instead of my own awareness. Interesting point of view that I have that point of view.

Allowance, leading to awareness, is a simple, effective way of dealing with the pains and unhappiness in your life. Other people's points of view on the subject simply divert you from having your own awareness.

You are not the only person on the planet who makes choices and shares them with others. Some of the choices that you might listen to could be shocking. "I'm going to sell my house and buy a swamp in Arizona! I'm so excited." How much allowance do you have when people are making the choice to kill their creations, like their house or to harm themselves in some way, like dying of thirst in the desert? Do you keep trying to find a way to fix them because you don't want their creations to die? Do you see the problem with this? What if they want their creations to die? Or to have their lives collapse? What if it's all a choice? *Their* choice! People think that "saving" someone would make them happy, but it usually doesn't. Saving them, in this sense, is often interpreted as your superiority overcoming their ineptitude. It begs the question, "Are you choosing to help because it makes you feel happy, or powerful, or beneficent?"

What judgments do you have about other people's ability to make their own choices that guide your actions here? When you stick your nose into even your best friend's affairs to save or heal him, you have positioned yourself above him as the all-wise beneficent.

You have to look at what you are trying to do there. If you are fighting for someone where they are not fighting for themselves, what does that create? You are left holding the hot potato.

You've got to look at what's actually going to work *for you*, not what you think should be. Choose to be in allowance of all the possibilities and ask what's going to create the most. Give yourself the gift of allowance to see what's going on.

A business owner chose to collaborate with some people who ended up creating a lot of havoc in his business. He was aware that something was not right, and he fired them. He didn't have any animosity or upset; he just got to the point where he told them, "You're not doing what I need. You've cost me a ton of money, and I'm not getting what I want. Goodbye!" He was in allowance of the money it cost him, and, ultimately, it gave him more awareness of what he will and will not allow somebody to do in the future. He looked at it and realized that it hadn't worked. It was crazy on his part because he was trusting people who were not trustworthy. He trusted what they said, not what they did. True allowance means looking at what somebody says and not just believing it, but recognizing that what they *do* is actually true. Allowance is not having blind faith that they will never lie. It is following your awareness. When he finally got clear that these people were not trustworthy, that he had set everything up so that they could lie to him, he said, "You're gone. Goodbye."

You see, he didn't try to control those people. He turned them loose to create whatever they were going to create. And slowly, but surely, they began to expose everything that was actually true for them. It seemed they thought he wasn't smart enough to notice the difference. Being in allowance of their opinion of him contributed to him being able to see what they were actually creating – and to choose what would work for what *he* desired to create. Allowance gives you the freedom to choose and create beyond the limitations everybody else thinks are true.

by. Interesting point of view allows you to move aside and let the attacker move on by, avoiding the pressure on you to buy a point of view.

I don't have a point of view that has to be right. I'm always willing to change, and I'm usually more interested in big changes than I am in little changes. But it can be the little changes you choose when you're totally willing to be aware of something that create a greater picture and a greater possibility. When you buy into somebody else's point of view, you're keeping one thing in place: their point of view. What if, instead, you had total choice?

I'm willing to listen to everybody's contribution without a point of view about it. Many people take the point of view that other people's points of view automatically have validity and make them a contribution. I don't have that point of view. I don't believe that people having a point of view makes them a contribution. Everybody has a point of view, but it is not necessarily something that will contribute to you.

Learn from others without buying their judgments and points of view.

Milton Keynes UK
Ingram Content Group UK Ltd.
UKHW031852260824
447357UK00001B/1